ARCHITECTURE IN MINUTES

SUSIE HODGE

ARCHITECTURE IN MINUTES

SUSIE HODGE

Quercus

CONTENTS

Introduction

Since the earliest days of human existence, structures have been made to provide shelter, warmth, refuge and privacy, and to facilitate worship, work and social interaction. In this respect, little has changed – but in terms of development, expression, interpretation and style, everything is in constant flux. This is what makes architecture so fascinating: although our essential requirements barely alter, different times, place and cultures have produced hugely varied buildings. The factors behind this variety include religious beliefs, availability of materials, variations in climate, limits of technology and economic systems. Among the most enduring works of architecture are castles, palaces and cathedrals, many of which are physical proof of technological progress. Buildings are not just about the way they look; they are also about how they function, their practicality, construction, decoration and how they fit into the landscape.

Architecture in Minutes is a brief introduction to some of the greatest architectural achievements of humankind. From the mysterious megaliths and spectacular pyramids of the ancient world, to the formidable fortresses and soaring Gothic churches of medieval Europe, and from elegant pagodas and magnificent mosques and palaces, to intricate urban developments and towering skyscrapers, this book surveys ideas, innovations and ingenuity. It considers society's changing requirements and expectations, as well as many of the architects who, through their knowledge of construction methods and materials and their understanding of proportion, aesthetics and local environments, have created unique and original buildings, instigating further change and developments over time.

In these pages, you will find iconic works of architecture, such as the Colosseum in Rome, the Parthenon in Athens and the Taj Mahal in Agra. Also explored are the architectural movements such as mannerism, neoclassicism and modernism, that put individual buildings into context, and certain exemplary architects, including Andrea Palladio, Frank Lloyd Wright and Le Corbusier. There are also lesser-known structures, movements and architects, providing an overview to consider, enjoy and hopefully inspire you to further investigate the fascinating world of architecture.

Megaliths

From around 5000 BCE, massive stone structures were erected across the world. Intended to be seen from great distances, the majority of megaliths (from the ancient Greek *megas* meaning 'great', and *lithos* meaning 'stone') are believed to have been used for religious rituals. Some, mainly in Turkey, Syria, Lebanon, Jordan and Saudi Arabia, probably related to farming.

The most famous and sophisticated surviving megalithic monument is Stonehenge on Salisbury Plain in Wiltshire, England (opposite), built in phases from around 3000 to 2000 BCE. Set in a precise stone circle, the giant stones are positioned with astronomical precision to align with rising and setting points of the Sun at specific times of year. The massive horizontal stone lintels and vertical posts are attached using the mortice-and-tenon technique, with carved protrusions on the uprights that fit neatly into slots on the lintels.

Mesopotamia and Persia

Predating the earliest known Egyptian buildings, the first permanent structures in the Near East were built in the area known as Mesopotamia from the tenth millennium BCE. The first culture to thrive in this region (between the Tigris and Euphrates rivers in present-day Iraq) were the Sumerians, followed by the Akkadians, the Assyrians, the Babylonians and finally the Persians, who conquered the area in 539 BCE. Among these civilizations' many accomplishments – including agriculture, a written language and the wheel – was the development of urban planning.

Architecture does not seem to have existed as an occupation, but the Mesopotamians perceived 'the craft of building' as a divine gift taught by the gods. They were the first society to build entire cities, dominated by ziggurats – tombs built to resemble the mountains where the gods lived. Cities were walled for protection, with large gateways. Mesopotamian buildings were initially made of mud bricks, but later of bricks fired in ovens.

Sumerian ruins at
Naffur, Iraq

Sumerian ziggurats

Ziggurats were stepped pyramids built for the worship of gods – at first by the Sumerians, but later by the Babylonians, Akkadians and Assyrians. Constructed in a stack of diminishing tiers on rectangular, oval or square bases, they had distinctive flat tops, and formed the focal point of Mesopotamian cities.

The oldest surviving ziggurat, in the ancient city of Uruk, pre-dates the Egyptian pyramids by several centuries. A shrine at the summit of the stepped platform was approached by outer stairs. The temple is believed to have been dedicated to the sky god Anu, and its corners point towards the cardinal points of the compass. Nearly a millennium later, during the Neo-Sumerian Empire, the ziggurat at Ur (opposite) was built c.2113–2096 BCE. The best preserved of the ancient ziggurats, it is built with a core of mud bricks and an outer casing of fired brick. Three converging ramps lead up to a platform, from which a central stairway continues to the top, where a temple once stood.

Egyptian pyramids

The pyramids were built as tombs for the rulers of Egypt's Old and Middle Kingdoms between c.2600 and 1800 BCE. Three types were built: step, bent and straight-sided. The most imposing are those at Giza (opposite), the largest of which was built for the pharaoh Khufu.

The pyramid shape is believed to have been favoured for the great heights that could be achieved, the notion of pointing directly up to the gods, and the commanding presence they created across the surrounding flat valleys. In a practical sense, fewer stones were required to be hauled to the top. These massive constructions – some rise up to 146 metres (450ft) while some of the blocks of limestone weigh 15 tonnes – were built with the utmost precision; the casing stones are so finely joined that a knife's edge cannot fit between them. Within, narrow passages lead to the royal burial chambers. Gypsum mortar held the blocks together, and the entire structures were encased in smooth white limestone quarried from the east bank of the River Nile, with the summit often topped in gold.

Ancient Egyptian temples

Built for the worship of gods, ancient Egyptian temples evolved from small shrines to large complexes. By the time of the New Kingdom (*c.*1550–1070 BCE), temples had become massive stone structures consisting of enclosed halls, open courts and entrance pylons. Certain parts could only be entered by priests, but the public visited other areas to pray, give offerings and seek guidance from the gods.

Notable examples include the Temple of Khons, built in 1198 BCE, with an avenue of sphinxes leading to an obelisk and hypostyle (columned) hall. Queen Hatshepsut's temple, designed by the architect Senenmut, was a geometric edifice dug into a rock face, built in 323 BCE. Its extended, double-colonnaded terraces are on three levels connected by ramps. The two Abu Simbel temples are also massive rock-cut structures, commissioned by Rameses II as monuments for himself (opposite) and his queen Nefertari. The entire complex was relocated in 1968 to avoid being submerged in Lake Nasser.

Assyrian fortifications and temples

The Assyrians (*c.*2500–539 BCE) were a warlike people for whom city fortifications served both a defensive and an ideological role: massive walls, representing the king's power, bore sculpted surfaces that displayed victories over enemies. The city of Nimrud boasted a palace set in vast courtyards, a ziggurat, the temple of Ezida and a huge encircling wall studded with towers. The final capital of the Assyrian Empire was the city of Nineveh (opposite), founded *c.*700 BCE on the Tigris River opposite the site of modern-day Mosul. King Sennacherib built a 12-kilometre (7.5-mile) brick wall around it with 15 towering gates, each named after an Assyrian god and each flanked by square towers with parapets and battlements.

Assyrians were a polytheistic people with a powerful priestly class. Their cities contained temples where their main gods were revered; as in Egyptian temples, gods were believed to live in sacred areas where only the priests could enter, and each god was represented by a specific statue in the temple.

Babylon

Built *c.*562 BCE, at its peak Babylon was by far the largest city of its time, with an area of at least 10 square kilometres (3.9 square miles). Set on the Euphrates River, its walls enclosed a densely packed area of shrines, temples, markets and houses, all grouped along grand avenues that were arranged in a grid. The city's Etemenanki Ziggurat (605–562 BCE) is believed to have inspired the biblical Tower of Babel. Part of a religious complex in the centre of the city, it was probably covered in coloured glazed bricks. Seven tiers rose from a square foundation 90-metres (297-ft) on each side, with a temple to the god Marduk at the top.

King Nebuchadnezzar II rebuilt the ziggurat as part of his reconstruction of Babylon in the sixth century BCE. He also built the Hanging Gardens – one of the seven wonders of the ancient world – for his wife, Amytis. The Ishtar Gate (opposite) was the largest and most breathtaking of eight entrances to the city. Finished with blue glazed bricks, it was decorated with reliefs of dragons, lions and young bulls.

Palace of Knossos

Decorated with frescoes on its walls depicting sports and religious ceremonies, the Palace of Knossos (built *c.*1700–1400 BCE) on the Aegean island of Crete was the ceremonial and political centre of Minoan civilization and culture, abandoned *c.*1380–1100 BCE. The palace complex was two storeys high and built around a large, open, square courtyard, comprising a maze of workrooms, living spaces and storerooms.

Colonnaded rooms were used for ceremonial purposes, and were usually on the first floor. Within, great columns were made not of stone, but of cypress tree trunks turned upside down and mounted on simple stone bases before being painted red. Although the palace has been immortalized in Greek mythology as the site of the Labyrinth (home of the half-man, half-bull Minotaur), it was actually well ventilated and light, with cool, sunlit rooms offering magnificent views. Yet there was no cohesive design to the rambling, extended building complex, which was added to over centuries of use.

Teotihuacán

In the broad San Juan valley to the northeast of modern-day Mexico City, at over 2,000 metres (7,000 ft) above sea level, stand the remains of Teotihuacán, once the largest and most powerful city in the pre-Columbian Americas. Who founded it, and when, remains something of a mystery, but its zenith was c.150 BCE–750 CE; the Aztec culture that arose more than a thousand years later considered Teotihuacán a sacred site and used ideas from its architecture for their own structures.

Organized in a strict grid, Teotihuacán once covered an area of up to 36 square kilometres (14 square miles). At its heart is a long, straight central avenue that the Aztecs called the Avenue of the Dead because the mounds lining its sides looked like tombs. The city's pyramids, incorporating ziggurat-style platforms, include the Pyramid of the Moon (c.250 CE) and Pyramid of the Sun (c.200 CE). The latter, standing over 61 metres (200 ft) high, was originally plastered and painted red, and chambers buried deep beneath it were possibly the site of ancient creation rituals.

Mayan

The influence of Teotihuacán (see page 24) reached the Mayan people in the tropical lowlands of what is now Guatemala. Their civilization reached its peak around the sixth century CE, with over 50 independent states and more stone cities than any other pre-Columbian culture. These included vast complexes of terraced temple-pyramids and palaces built around large plazas.

With a population of about 45,000, the city of Tikal featured great plazas with many stone temples built on platforms, including wide staircases and painted stucco façades. The largest of these was the Temple of the Inscriptions (built c.700–800 CE) – a massive stone rectangle with a steep staircase leading up nine levels. The tall, narrow Temple of the Giant Jaguar, built c.730, rises in nine steep tiers of finely carved stone. Roof combs, or cresteria, crowned many Mayan pyramids. At Uxmal, a Mayan city whose name translates as 'thrice built', the Palace of the Governors (opposite, c.900) is a trio of wide, low buildings connected by triangular stone arches.

Inca

A t its peak from 1438 to 1532 CE, the vast Inca Empire stretched 4,000 kilometres (2,500 miles) from Peru to Chile and across to the Amazon rainforests. Incan accomplishments in civil engineering were outstanding, but because they did not write, their history remains obscure. Most of their ceremonial architecture was built to worship the sun god and his temporal representative, 'Inca'. Elements of their buildings include wall reliefs, terracing, trapezoidal openings and masks. Chan Chan was the capital of the pre-Incan kingdom of Chimor, built c.1200–1470. With reservoirs and an irrigation system, it was arranged on nine quadrangles, within which hundreds of near-identical mud brick buildings were organized. At an altitude of 2,430 metres (7,970 ft) above sea level, the granite-walled city of Machu Picchu (opposite) was built in the mid-1400s from local materials. Terraces, containing courtyards, gardens and fields, are noted for their mortar-free masonry: though extraordinarily close-fitting, the loose stone blocks permitted slight movement, which helped them survive earthquakes.

The Greek orders

By the fifth century BCE, Greek architecture had attained a purity of style, harmony and technical expertise. A century earlier, architects and stonemasons had developed a system of rules to use in all buildings. These rules became known as the orders, and are most easily seen in the styles of their columns.

A Greek column, normally comprising a capital, shaft and base, came in three types. The Doric, uniquely, has no base, and the fluted shaft rises up to a plain convex capital. Examples can be seen in the Parthenon. The Ionic is taller and slimmer, with flat bands separating the flutes on the shaft; there may be figurative reliefs around the base, and a female 'caryatid' figure may stand in place of a fluted shaft. Ionic capitals have two pairs of scroll-like volutes, with architraves that consist of three horizontal planes, each projecting slightly, and a plain or sculptured frieze. Similar to Ionic but more ornate, Corinthian capitals are often decorated with carved acanthus leaves and four scrolls, or sometimes with carved lotus or palm leaves.

Ancient Greek temples and theatres

Using a structural system of vertical columns and horizontal beams, the Greeks ensured architectural consistency and visual harmony. Their most important buildings were temples, closely followed by theatres, built on a range of scales.

The tiny temple of Athena Nike, built *c.*421 BCE to overlook Athens on one side and face the Acropolis on the other, has four Ionic columns to front and back, inspired by natural sources including rams' horns, shells and Egyptian lotus flowers. In contrast the temple of Concordia (440–430 BCE) at Agrigento, Sicily (opposite), is a well-preserved example of the Doric order. The massive temple of Artemis at Ephesus (*c.*356 BCE), one of the seven wonders of the ancient world, was reached by steps flanked with bronze Amazonian warrior statues. Its central span of more than 80 metres (260 ft) was supported by almost 120 gold-coated Ionic columns. The theatre of Epidaurus (350 BCE) is an immense amphitheatre 118 metres (387 ft) across, with banked tiers of limestone seats and superb acoustic qualities.

The Acropolis

The temples on the Acropolis, a sacred rocky hill dedicated to Athena on the outskirts of Athens, represent the pinnacle of Greek architectural achievement. The hill had been inhabited as far back as the fifth millennium BCE, but Pericles (c.495–429 BCE) ordered and coordinated the construction of the site's most important buildings, including the Parthenon, the Propylaea, the Erechtheion and the Temple of Athena Nike.

The sculptor Phidias (480–430 BCE) planned the layout for visual drama and spatial harmony, and most of the architecture was built in the Doric order, with slender columns and lavishly decorated friezes. A grand stairway leads to the marble columns of the Propylaea, a road for carts and sacrificial beasts, marking the entrance to the holiest area of the Acropolis. Behind the Propylaea stood a 9-metre (30-ft) bronze statue of Athena Promachus, while the elegant marble Temple of Erechtheion (c.420–393 BCE), built on a sloping site, has an entrance lined with six monumental caryatids (columns in the form of female figures), and two porches.

The Parthenon

Generally viewed as the archetypal Greek temple, the Parthenon (*c.*432 BCE) was designed by Ictinus, Callicrates and Phidias, and dedicated to the virgin (*parthenos*) goddess Athena, patron of Athens. Though it has some Ionic features, it is mainly Doric, with dimensions in the Doric length–breadth ratio of 9:4. Beneath its painted and gilded roof was a massive gold and ivory sculpture of Athena. While most Greek temples had six columns across the front, the Parthenon had eight. A total of 46 outer supporting columns of marble stood over 10 metres (33 ft) high; they are Doric, with simple capitals and fluted shafts, and the stylobate (column platform) is gently curved to shed rainwater and add strength. To compensate for the optical illusion of dead-straight columns appearing thin-waisted, the architects thickened them – a subtle distortion known as *entasis*. Above the architrave of the entablature was a frieze of 92 metopes (marble panels), while across the lintels of the inner columns runs a continuous frieze in low relief, comprising one of the Ionic elements of the building.

Greek architectural sculpture

Greek architects used a complex mix of optical illusions, ratios and rigid structural rules. The overall appearance of their buildings was intentionally simple, but sculptural decorations were often elaborate. Forming a key element of many temples and monuments, they featured on column capitals and pediments, in friezes and as statues.

Exterior sculpture usually featured in the metopes and triglyphs (two alternating panel types) of the entablature, the roof-supporting structure that sat across the columns. Some late Doric temples featured a continuous frieze around the outer wall of the cella (inner temple chamber), but the Ionic period, from the mid-sixth century BCE, brought more intricate decorations, including reliefs that often showed historicla or mythological narratives. Around the Parthenon's cella, a low-relief frieze depicts the people of Athens in a Panathenaic procession, a key local celebration. Greek buildings and sculpture were always vividly painted, and often further embellished with metal accessories.

Greek urban planning

The first historical figure to be associated with urban planning was the architect, physician, mathematician, meteorologist and philosopher Hippodamus of Miletus (498–408 BCE). His plans for Greek cities were characterized by order and regularity, with straight, parallel streets laid out in rational grid systems, and functions grouped together in certain areas (something rare at the time, since any invaders would be able to find their way about by following this logic). Hippodamus planned the cities of Miletus (opposite), Priene and Lynthus, creating neatly ordered and organized cities with wide streets.

Shrines, theatres, government buildings, markets and the agora (a central space where athletic, political, artistic and spiritual activities took place) were all grouped together in central zones, and land use was divided into the sacred, public and private (mirroring Hippodamus's division of the citizenry into three classes). Housing was the final area to be zoned, after all the other areas were allocated.

Stupas and temples

During the third century BCE, religious architecture developed in the Indian subcontinent with three types of structures: monasteries (viharas), shrines (stupas) and prayer halls (chaityas or chaitya grihas). Following changes in religious practice, stupas were gradually incorporated into prayer halls. These reached their zenith in the first millennium CE, particularly in the cave complexes of Ajanta and Ellora (see page 48).

Evolving from burial mounds, the stupa developed as a brick and plaster hemisphere with a pointed superstructure, often enshrining relics of the Buddha and acting as a sacred centre for rituals. The most famous surviving example is the Great Stupa at Sanchi from the first century BCE. These simple structures later evolved into complex Hindu temples, richly ornamented, often encrusted with sculpture, and sometimes also brightly painted. Noted examples are the temples of Angkor Wat (c.1100) in Cambodia (see page 88), and Phra Prang Sam Yod in Thailand (c.1300, opposite).

The Great Wall of China

The largest military structure in the world stretches some 6,500 kilometres (4,000 miles) from Shanhaiguan in the east to Jiayuguan in the west. The Great Wall is an amalgam of ancient walls from over 20 states and dynasties, first united into a single defensive system in 214 BCE under the rule of Emperor Qin Shi Huang (260–210 BCE), and later rebuilt three more times to protect against invasion. Varying in height from 6 to 10 metres (20 to 33 ft), the wall has an average depth of 6.5 metres (21 ft) at its base, tapered to 5.8 metres (19 ft) at the top.

Original local materials included stone, brick, rammed earth and wood, but the third rebuilding of the wall (from the ascent of the Ming dynasty in 1368 through to its conclusion in 1644) was stronger and more complex than any of the others. The eastern half is built of dressed stone or kiln-fired brick, the western half of rammed earth, sometimes faced with sun-dried brick. Watchtowers, gateways and forts along the length of the wall guarded against approaching raiders.

Pagodas

Tiered towers with multiple eaves, Chinese pagodas evolved from multi-storey timber towers created before the arrival of Buddhism in the first century CE, but share a heritage with Indian stupas. Primarily built of wood or brick, the structures themselves were hollow – their main function was to house religious relics beneath the ground, although a few were built in scenic isolation as elements of *feng shui*, and some began to appear on palaces as decorative features. Most early examples, built before the tenth century, had square bases, but later versions were built on polygonal plans. The shapes of the eaves and decorative details varied with time and location, while tiers changed from straight to an upwardly curving style dating from the 12th century. The earliest surviving Chinese timber pagoda is the White Horse Temple in Luoyang (founded 68 CE, rebuilt in the 13th century), while the oldest brick pagoda is the 12-sided Songyue monastery (523 CE, opposite). Buddhists introduced pagodas to Japan in the seventh century CE. They are highly resistant to earthquakes, owing to their structural flexibility.

Cave temples

Dating from the second century BCE to about 460–480 CE, some 30 rock-cut Buddhist cave temples were built at Ajanta, near the city of Aurangabad in the Indian state of Maharashtra. Nearby lie the Ellora caves (opposite), built during the sixth to ninth centuries by the Rashtrakuta dynasty and comprising Hindu, Buddhist and Jain temples. The Badami cave temples in the Bagalkot district, meanwhile, comprise four caves, all carved out of the soft sandstone cliff.

Today some 1,200 Indian cave temples survive, built chiefly between the fifth and tenth centuries, in fairly close proximity to each other. Relics from a period marked by religious harmony, most caves consist of viharas or monasteries: multi-storey buildings carved high up and deep inside mountains, comprising living quarters, kitchens, prayer halls and verandas. They feature complex construction methods, with integral pillars, intricate room systems and fine, detailed carving – not to mention the accurate removal of thousands of tonnes of rock.

Petra

Hidden from the outside world for hundreds of years, the Nabataean caravan city of Petra lay at an important crossroads on trading routes between Arabia, Egypt and Syria–Phoenicia. At the height of their power, the Nabataeans were a wealthy and powerful people controlling vast expanses of desert located in present-day Jordan. Tucked away between desert canyons and mountains, the capital of their empire was half-built, half-carved from rose-coloured sandstone between 400 BCE and 106 CE.

An ingenious water management system allowed Petra to thrive in an otherwise arid area: dwellings were simple, while civic and religious architecture was a blend of Assyrian, Egyptian, Greek and Roman influences. Façades blend simplicity and opulence with columns and carvings: the huge Khazreh or Treasury, tomb of King Aretas III (r.85–62 BCE), incorporates Corinthian and Nabataean columns (opposite), as well as friezes carved from solid rock, and figures from both Nabataean and Greek mythology.

Cement

Lacking the extensive quarries of marble available to the Greeks, the Romans had to create their own durable building material. The ancient Egyptians had used gypsum plaster (though this was not particularly strong), the Mesopotamians used bitumen, and some Greek builders, particularly on the coast of Turkey, had developed a form of cement around 200 BCE – but the Romans perfected it.

The Roman invention was distinguished by the addition of lime, which binds sand, water and clay, and by increasing use of finely ground volcanic lava (from Pozzuoli, near Naples) in place of clay. The resulting 'pozzolanic' cement was the strongest mortar in use prior to the British development of Portland cement in the mid-18th century. Roman concrete was based on a hydraulic-setting cement, which set and became adhesive due to a chemical reaction between its dry ingredients and water. By adding fragments of volcanic rubble to this mixture, the Romans were able to build their great feats of engineering.

Concrete dome
of the Pantheon,
Rome

Vitruvius

Marcus Vitruvius Pollio (*c*.75–*c*.15 BCE) was a Roman architect, civil and military engineer who became known for his work *De Architectura*, or *The Ten Books on Architecture*. As the only surviving major work on architecture from classical antiquity, *De Architectura* is an important source of modern knowledge about Roman building methods, as well as planning and design. It had a huge influence on the artists and architects of the Renaissance, and for centuries influenced major buildings around the world.

Vitruvius asserted that a structure must exhibit the three qualities of *firmitas, utilitas et venustas* – firmness, commodity and delight. In other words, the ideal building is sturdy, useful and beautiful. Discussions on dimensions and ratios culminated in Vitruvius rationalizing the proportions of the human body. This 'Vitruvian Man' was later drawn by Leonardo da Vinci (1452–1519) as a figure within a circle and a square, the fundamental geometric shapes of the cosmic order.

MARCUS VITRUVIUS ROMAN.

Architectus antiqus Cæs. Augusti.

Roman engineering

The Romans built an empire that began with a few Italian states and spread to encompass most of Europe in the west, and to the Persian Empire in the east. They established their dominance in part through law-making, but also through developing advanced engineering techniques that enabled them to build straight roads irrespective of natural features, cities planned on rigid grids, aqueducts, viaducts, bridges, baths, arches and domes. Although some of their inventions and techniques simply improved on earlier (often Greek) ideas, their accomplishments surpassed any other civilization of the time.

Concrete made possible the construction of great vaults and domes, some of whose spans were not equalled until the development of steel in the 19th century. Amphitheatres allowed hundreds of spectators to see and hear spectacular displays, plays and special effects. Aqueducts, built from arches in one, two and three tiers, carried water in cement-lined channels, which ran along the upper level before diverting into pipes.

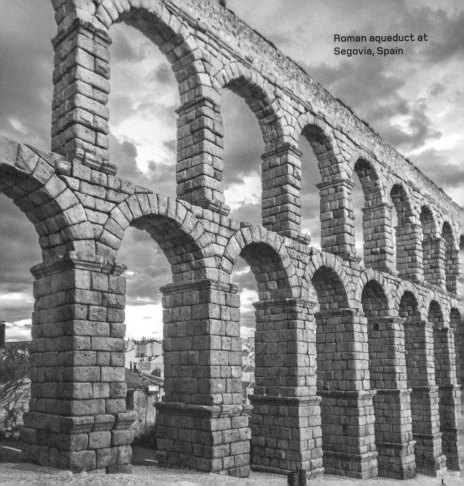

Roman aqueduct at
Segovia, Spain

Arches, orders and inscriptions

Using free-standing columns as stabilizers, the Romans developed the rounded stone arch. Arches are often used to support large expanses of wall, and for building foundations. They are built upwards from either side using a temporary wooden frame, and the final stone to be dropped into the centre of a span is the keystone. From arches, the Romans also developed arcades (a series of arches on columns) and the barrel vault, cross vault and dome. They used five orders on their columns. To the Greek Doric, Ionic and Corinthian (see page 30), they added the Tuscan (an even simpler form of Doric) and the Composite, a richer form of Corinthian.

Columns and passageways were decorated with reliefs and free-standing sculptures. Some triumphal arches were surmounted by a statue or a *currus triumphalis*, a group of statues of the emperor or general. Inscriptions had finely cut letters, carefully designed for maximum clarity and simplicity, with no decorative flourishes, emphasizing a Roman taste for restraint.

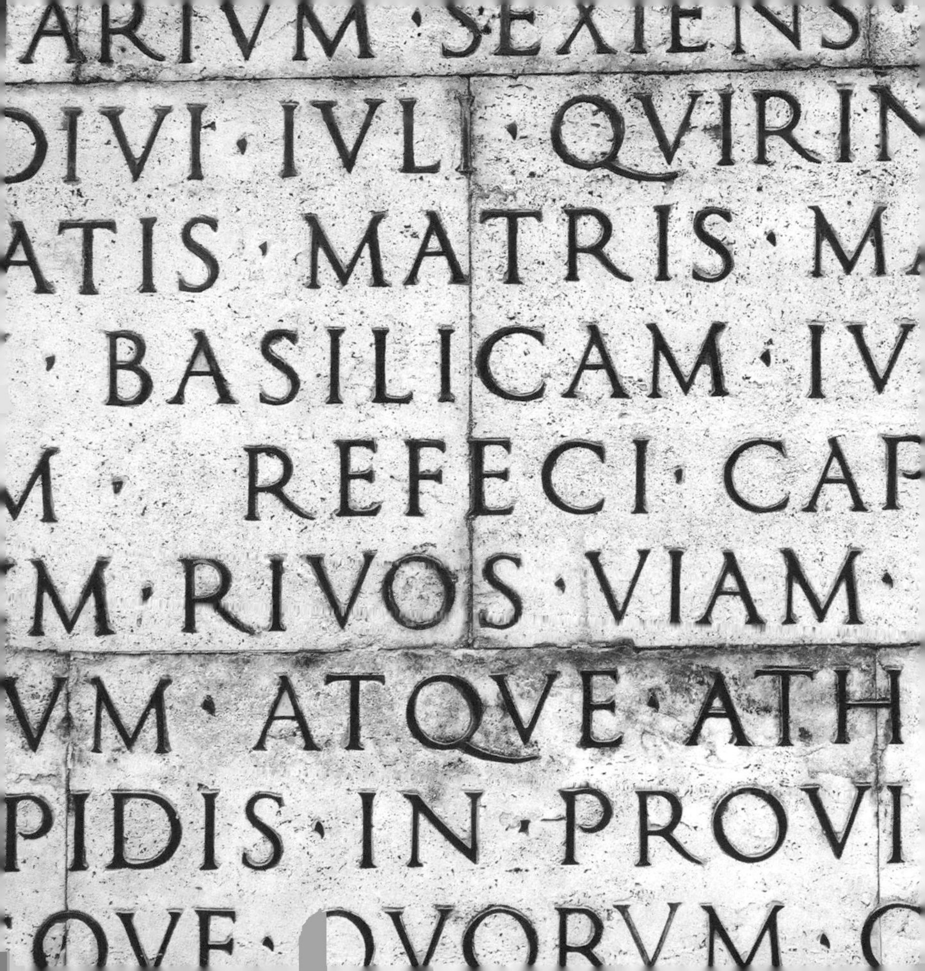
ARIVM·SEXIENS
DIVI·IVLI·QVIRIN
ATIS·MATRIS·MA
·BASILICAM·IV
M·REFECI·CAP
M·RIVOS·VIAM·
VM·ATQVE·ATH
PIDIS·IN·PROVI
QVE·QVORVM·C

The Pont du Gard

Crossing the River Gard in the South of France, the Pont du Gard is part of the Nîmes aqueduct, built *c.*40–50 CE to carry water from a spring at Uzès to the Roman city of Nemausus (Nîmes). General Marcus Agrippa, son-in-law and aide of Emperor Augustus, is credited with its conception. Although the direct distance between the two is only about 20 kilometres (12 miles), the aqueduct takes a winding route of about 50 kilometres (30 miles) to avoid the Garrigue hills above Nîmes. The tallest of all elevated Roman aqueducts, the Pont du Gard has three tiers of arches, and rises to a height of 48.8 metres (160 ft).

The first tier is composed of six arches, each 15–24 metres (51–80 ft) wide, with the largest spanning the river; the second tier has 11 arches of similar dimensions; while the third, carrying the conduit, consists of 35 smaller arches, each spanning 4.5 metres (15 ft). Like many ancient Roman structures, the Pont du Gard was built without mortar, and is a great example of the precision that Roman engineers were able to achieve.

Roman bridges

To create structures strong enough to span large distances, while bearing heavy loads and remaining stable, the Romans constructed voussoir arches with keystones. Voussoirs were wedge-shaped or tapered blocks of stone placed in semi-circular arrangements; to each side, the arch rested on piers or columns of stone blocks mortared with pozzolanic cement. The weight of the stone and concrete in the bridge itself compressed the tapered stones together, making the arch extremely strong. Voussoir arches were the basis for both single-span bridges and lengthy multi-arched aqueducts. Some early Roman arch bridges, influenced by the ancient notion of the ideal form of the circle, are made from a full circle, with the stone arch continuing underground. However, once engineers realised that an arch did not even have to be semicircular to remain stable, some later structures featured 'segmental' arches encompassing only a smaller arc of the circle. The Romans were also the first – and, until the Industrial Revolution, only – engineers to construct concrete bridges.

Roman bridge at Giornico,
Switzerland

Roman temples

B ased on Greek and Etruscan forerunners, Roman temples generally centred on a main room, or cella, housing the icon of the deity to whom the temple was dedicated (and often a small altar for incense or libations). Behind this lay one or more rooms used by temple attendants for offerings. Public religious ceremonies occurred *outside* the temple building; unlike Greek temples, which looked the same from all aspects, each Roman temple had a columned portico along its front.

The most important temple in ancient Rome was the Temple of Jupiter (509 BCE), which stood on the Capitoline Hill surrounded by a precinct where assemblies met and statues and victory trophies were displayed. After the original wooden temple burned down, it was rebuilt using Greek marble columns and covered in gold and mosaic. The circular Temple of Vesta (*c.*100 BCE, opposite) is the oldest surviving marble building in Rome, with 20 Corinthian columns. Despite its name, it is believed to have been dedicated to Hercules Olivarius, patron god of olive oil merchants.

The Colosseum

The largest amphitheatre ever built was constructed in Rome in 72–80 CE, to host public spectacles including gladiator fights, wild animal hunts and public executions. The Colosseum was part of a wider construction programme begun by Emperor Vespasian to restore Rome's glory prior to the recent civil war. Like nothing ever built, it dominated the city and became a symbol of Rome, its society and culture. Oval in shape, made from locally quarried travertine stone, brick, volcanic stone and pumice, it also featured concrete, then a recent invention. The Colosseum had four tiers, with 80 monumental open arcades on three of them, and statues in each. The first floor had Doric columns, the second Ionic, and the top floor featured Corinthian pilasters (column-like reliefs on walls) and small windows. On each tier, passages and corridors had vaulted concrete ceilings on limestone supports. At over 45 metres (150 ft) high and 545 metres (1,780 ft) in perimeter, the Colosseum held some 50,000 spectators, who could be evacuated in 15 minutes.

The Pantheon

Built by the Emperor Hadrian c.128 CE, the Pantheon covered a temple erected by the Emperor Augustus's son-in-law, Marcus Agrippa, in 27 BCE. The exterior, fronted by a portico of granite Corinthian columns (eight wide, three deep), leads to a huge rotunda. The spectacular dome, a half-sphere of 44.3 metres (144 ft) in diameter, is exactly equal to its floor to summit height. The 8-metre (27-ft) oculus, or 'open eye', at its crown is the main source of light. In the dome, sunken panels, or coffers, create interest, but also serve to hollow out the concrete and reduce its load on the brick supporting wall. The use of low-density rock, such as pumice, in the upper parts of the dome also reduces weight. With a series of restraining arches, the wall features alternating, curved and squared recesses. Overall, it is an open, airy, unified space. Pantheon means 'all the gods', and in 609 it became the first temple to be consecrated as a Catholic church, renamed the Church of Santa Maria ad Martyres. The remains of many Christian martyrs were brought from the catacombs and buried beneath its floor.

Basilicas, secular and sacred

The Roman public hall or basilica is a rectangular building with side aisles behind rows of supporting columns. The oldest-known example was built in Pompeii in the second century BCE. Originally, the basilica was a hall of justice or commercial exchange; tribunals took place in the apse (a recess at one end), and offerings were made at the altar before business began. In 313 CE, Constantine recognized Christianity, and by 326 it had become the official religion of the Roman Empire. The three great churches founded by Constantine in Rome are all basilicas. Two of them, St Peter's and St Paul's, feature the transept, which crossed the nave near the altar end and gave more space for pilgrims or clergy. (It also turned the ground plan into the shape of a Christian cross.) Nave, aisles, transept and apse became common elements of rectangular Western churches. When Constantine moved the new capital of Rome to Byzantium, renaming it Constantinople, the empire stretched from Milan and Cologne to Syria, Greece and Egypt, building basilicas everywhere that reflected local ideas.

Ruins of the second-century Severan Basilica at Leptis Magna, a Roman city in modern Libya

Roman towns and cities

Wherever the Roman armies conquered, they established towns and cities, extending the empire and, with it, their architectural and engineering achievements. Local materials were used, but common elements prevailed, including straight roads, arched bridges and aqueducts. Roman towns were designed in grids, centring on the crossing of two main roads, one oriented north–south and the other east–west. Where they met, the main buildings and spaces were set up, including the basilica, forum, market, amphitheatre, baths and temple. Dwellings filled the straight streets leading off the main roads. There was also an army barracks in every town, protected by a fortified surrounding wall, while aqueducts provided clean water and a sewage disposal system removed waste. The most well known of these towns and cities are Rome itself, Pompeii and Herculaneum, although Pompeii did not conform to a Roman grid as it had to fit into mountainous terrain. Private houses were typically 'inward-looking', opening onto a central courtyard, though many Pompeiian houses also had balconies.

Roman ruins at Ostia Antica, Italy

Roman baths

Roman houses had water supplied via lead pipes, but as water supply was taxed, public baths, or *thermae*, evolved. These took on monumental proportions, with colonnades, arches and domes, statues and mosaics. Features included the *apodyterium* (changing rooms), *palaestrae* (exercise rooms), *notatio* (open-air swimming pool), *laconica* and *sudatoria* (heated dry and wet sweating-rooms), the *caldarium*, *tepidarium* and *frigidarium* (hot, warm and cool rooms), and chambers for massage and other treatments, toilets, libraries and a range of other facilities.

Early baths were heated by braziers, later using the hypocaust system, in which wood-burning furnaces sent warm air under a raised floor. The introduction of glass windows from the first century CE improved temperature control. Water was supplied by purpose-built aqueducts and regulated by huge internal reservoirs. Notable examples include the Baths of Caracalla and Diocletian in Rome (*c.*215 and *c.*305 CE respectively), and the complex in Bath in England (second century CE, opposite).

Library of Celsus

The Library of Celsus at Ephesus was named after the city's former Roman governor, Gaius Julius Celsus Polemaeanus, whose tomb lies beneath its ground floor. Completed *c.*117 CE, it was a repository of over 12,000 manuscript scrolls, stored in niches around the walls on three galleried floors. Double walls behind the scroll niches protected them from the extremes of temperature and humidity, and there was also an auditorium for lectures or presentations.

Corinthian-style columns front the ground floor, whose three entrances are echoed by three windows in the upper storey. By making the columns at the sides of the façade shorter than those at the centre, the architects created the illusion of a larger building. Above the door stood a statue of Athena, goddess of wisdom, while statues flanking the front entrances represent wisdom (Sophia), knowledge (Episteme), intelligence (Ennoia) and valour (Arete): the virtues of Celsus. Reliefs are carved on the façade, while the interior was paved with decorated marble.

Constantine

onstantine I the Great (272–337 CE) was the last pagan and first Christian emperor of Rome, initiating his empire's conversion to Christianity and the development of Byzantine culture. Early architectural commissions, such as the Baths of Constantine in Rome, reflect the pagan past, but others, such as the Aula Palatina at Trier in Germany, are Christian. As well as the great church of St Peter, his achievements include the completion of the huge Basilica Nova, modelled on the frigidaria (cold rooms) of bath complexes, and the Arch of Constantine (opposite), commemorating victory over his rival Maxentius. Built of marble blocks and brickwork riveted with marble, the arch is 21 metres (69 ft) high, 26 metres (85 ft) wide and 7.4 metres (24 ft) deep. Each façade features four Corinthian columns of yellow Numidean marble, as well as decorations salvaged from as far back as the Emperor Trajan (98–117 CE). In 324, Constantine founded Constantinople as the 'new Rome', and his interest in building found expression there in the churches of the Holy Wisdom (see page 80) and of the Apostles.

Hagia Sophia

Rebuilt on the orders of Byzantine emperor Justinian from 537 CE after the original burnt to the ground, Constantinople's Hagia Sophia, or Church of the Holy Wisdom, was one of the most lavish and expensive buildings of all time. Designed by scientists Anthemius of Tralles and Isidore of Miletus, it took more than 10,000 workmen five years to build.

Its greatest triumph is a 32.5-metre (107-ft) dome, raised over a square central space using tapering triangular elements known as pendentives. This technique allowed the builders to dispense with supporting walls, instead using half-domes to the east and west to hold up the main dome (heavy reinforcing buttresses were added later). The dome was overlaid in gold to evoke Heaven, with the square space below laid in coloured marble symbolizing Earth. With the decline of the Byzantine Empire, the building was ransacked several times, and when the Ottoman Turks stormed Constantinople in 1453, Sultan Mehmed II converted it into a mosque, with minarets added over the next century.

Byzantine architecture

When Constantine established Constantinople in 324 CE, the Roman Empire split in two, with a capital city for each half: Constantinople in the east and Ravenna in the west. The subsequent fusing of Greek and Roman styles in the Byzantine (Eastern Roman) Empire led to forms such as the Greek-cross plan church, with its four equal arms, square centre and dome roof. Important buildings featured high ceilings and opulent decoration including marble, mosaics and inlays, although churches tended to feature painted icons in place of statues.

With Constantinople located on so many major trade routes, Byzantine architecture spread across a vast area, influencing medieval, Renaissance and Ottoman styles. Surviving examples include the octagonal basilica of San Vitale in Ravenna (opposite, 547 CE), whose Byzantine elements include a polygonal apse, capitals, narrow bricks and rich mosaics; St Mark's Cathedral in Venice (1092); and the churches of Hosios Loukas (Saint Luke) in Boeotia, Greece, founded in the 11th century.

Hindu temples

The earliest Hindu temples were constructed in the fourth to fifth centuries CE. Over the ensuing years, they were built in many variations, adapted to the worship of different deities and to regional beliefs. Despite their differences, all were open, symmetrical constructions, built on square grids. Each temple comprises an inner sanctum and the *garbhagriha* or 'womb-chamber', housing the image of the primary idol or deity. Above the *garbhagriha* is the tower-like *shikhara*, or *vimana*, and an ambulatory for *parikrama* (circumambulation). Another staple is a congregation hall, and sometimes an antechamber and porch. The earliest examples were made of clay with roofs thatched with straw or leaves; later, brick and stone were used.

The Hindu culture encouraged creative independence, but architects and builders nonetheless had to adhere to certain 'rules', including precise and harmonious geometry throughout, tall towers, and ornate sculptures of gods, worshippers, erotic scenes, animals, and floral and geometric patterns.

Hindu temple at Khajuraho,
Madhya Pradesh, c. 1000 CE

Prambanan

A ninth-century temple complex in Indonesia on the borders of Yogyakarta and Central Java, Prambanan is the largest Hindu temple in ancient Java. It was probably built to mark the return of the Hindu Sañjaya dynasty to power in Central Java after nearly a century of dominance by the Buddhist Sailendra dynasty. The Sañjaya king Rakai Pikatan founded it *c.*850 CE to honour Lord Shiva, and subsequent kings expanded it into a compound of three zones. The outer zone was a large open space; the middle zone contains 224 small, identical shrines; the central, holiest zone is surrounded by a square stone wall with a gate at each of the four cardinal points. The three main *trimurti* (shrines) within this walled compound include the Shiva shrine at centre, on top of a terraced and richly decorated plinth. Reliefs illustrating stories from the *Ramayana* epic continue on the terraces of the Brahma and Vishnu shrines. Though it is complex, Prambanan nonetheless conforms to Hindu temple design requirements in following a geometric grid dominated by the imposing 47-metre (154-ft) central building.

Angkor Wat

The city of Angkor, built by the Hindu Khmer kings of northwest Cambodia between the 9th and 15th centuries, contains the monumental complex of Angkor Wat – the world's largest religious monument – constructed by King Suryavarman (r.1113–45) as a temple to the god Vishnu and as a royal mausoleum. It is laid out to symbolize the universe: the central structure represents the holy Mount Meru, home to the Hindu gods; the five surrounding towers are the mountain peaks that were thought to mark the edge of the cosmos; and the broad moat represents the oceans believed to lie beyond.

The main temple building has three tiered terraces that represent earth, water and wind. The many bas-reliefs that adorn the buildings are detailed representations of Hindu mythology. It is an act of veneration to circumambulate a Hindu temple, and the ambulatory of Angkor Wat amounts to 19 kilometres (12 miles). The complex was later copied across the Khmer Empire, but no other Hindu temple attained such scale and precision.

Japanese temples

Japanese Shinto shrines are dwellings for the gods, the *kami*. Sacred objects that represent them may be stored out of sight in the *honden*, or inner sanctuary, but a *honden* may not be present if there are altar-like structures called *himorogi* nearby. Buddhist temples also exist alongside Shinto shrines, with both sharing some features of Japanese traditional architecture (although Buddhist architecture was brought to Japan from China and other Asian cultures, and so is somewhat eclectic).

Partly due to these diverse origins and partly in response to the differing climates across Japan, shrines vary in structure, but some features recur. Most Japanese temples are made of wood to be earthquake-proof, and, although borrowing from Chinese architectural designs, have their own distinctive characteristics. Gently curving roofs are common, supported by a post-and-lintel structure, with walls that are paper-thin and often movable, making inner spaces fluid.

Toshogu Shrine at Nikko, 1617

Hōryū-ji temple and pagoda

The first temple and pagoda at Hōryū-ji in Nara Prefecture was built in 607 CE, soon after Buddhism reached Japan. Struck by lightning in 670, it was rebuilt c.711, and repaired on several occasions. Its perimeter is a covered wooden corridor with an inner gateway (*chumon*) leading into the temple courtyard. Japanese design and architecture emphasizes harmony with nature, and Hōryū-ji, although following Chinese pagodas, focuses on a Japanese understanding of grace, unity and asymmetry.

The complex comprises a five-storey pagoda, the Golden Hall (*kondo*), a free-standing lecture hall (*kodo*), and several small pavilions that were used for housing the sutras, or sacred texts. The pagoda contained symbolic relics of the Buddha, while the Golden Hall was a storehouse of religious images. The pagoda's graceful flaring eaves are supported by cantilevered cloud-pattern bracket arms. With no means to ascend to the upper levels, its function is simply to add decorative height to the overall appearance.

Song Dynasty

With towering Buddhist pagodas, great stone and wooden bridges, lavish tombs and extravagant palaces, China's Song Dynasty (960–1279) became noted for its sophisticated building developments, such as the 110-metre (360-ft) pagoda in Bianjing, capital of the Northern Song. Cities such as Bianjing were built on square or rectangular plans, with walls of rammed earth topped by a mixture of broken brick, tiles and crushed stone.

Pagodas developed from purely wooden structures to stone, brick and even cast iron. The Iron Pagoda of Yuquan Temple in Hubei Province (built c.1061) incorporates 53 tonnes of cast metal in its 21.3-metre (70-ft) structure. The Liuhe or 'Six Harmonies' Pagoda in the Southern Song capital of Hangzhou, in Zhejiang Province, is another fine example of pagoda architecture from the time (opposite). Standing 60 metres (197 ft) tall, it was built with a red-brick frame and 13 stages of wooden eaves. Internally, however, the pagoda has just seven stories, each with an elaborately decorated ceiling.

Early Islamic design

The Umayyads (r.661–750) were the first Islamic rulers to found a dynasty, and their magnificent buildings were designed to project authority, combining elements of Byzantine and Sassanid Persian architecture. Establishing their court at Damascus, they built a series of grand palaces.

The Great Mosque (opposite, 705–15), modelled on the prototype of the Prophet's mosque in Mecca, featured a vast enclosed courtyard with a minaret at each corner, and a central prayer hall divided by Corinthian columns into three aisles. Drawing on Christian architectural features, it included domes, round arches, Byzantine-style gold mosaics, carved reliefs and veined marble slabs. The Great Mosque at Samarra (851) is noted for its spiralling minaret, the 52-metre (162-ft) Malwiya Tower, as well as early Islamic decoration in the form of floral and geometric stucco carvings. The Great Mosque of Córdoba, built in 785 under the Abbasid caliphate (750–1513), marked the beginnings of Moorish architecture in the Iberian peninsula.

The Dome of the Rock

Completed in 691–2 CE by the Umayyad Caliph Abd Al-Malik, the Dome of the Rock is a shrine on Temple Mount in Jerusalem; the earliest surviving Muslim monumental building (albeit with a few alterations), it is one of the city's defining landmarks. The site is important for Jews, Christians and Muslims, and the Dome replaces earlier temples on the location. It was initially intended to stand as a substitute for the Kaaba, the shrine of the great mosque at Mecca.

The octagonal plan was probably based on the Byzantine Chapel of St Mary, built in 451–8 CE on the road between Jerusalem and Bethlehem. Mounted on an elevated drum, the great dome is 20 metres (66 ft) in diameter and 20.5 metres (67 ft) high. It rises above 12 columns and 4 piers, with an octagonal walkway of 16 columns and 8 piers. Light pours in through 16 windows evenly spaced around the drum, and 40 more in the lower, octagonal part. It has been claimed that around 100,000 gold coins were melted down for the dome's original exterior.

Islamic urban planning

The spread of Islam to parts of Asia, Africa and Europe had an overwhelming impact on urban development. With great diversity in climate, building forms and construction materials, there was at first no uniform style, but the Fatimid period in Egypt (969–1171) saw the emergence of a common architectural vocabulary and town planning.

The main mosque lay at the heart of each town, usually close to the *suq* (market). Nearby was the *madrasa* (school or college), and also the *casbah*, or citadel – the governor's walled palace. Beyond lay residential quarters. In hot and arid climates, residences were designed around courtyards that preserved privacy and kept interiors cool. Doors were located so that they did not overlook others, and windows placed higher than passers-by. Similarly, high windows in buildings did not overlook other dwellings or courtyards. The different quarters were connected by narrow winding streets, with tombs and cemeteries located a short distance beyond the town walls.

The Great Mosque of Kairouan
and surroundings, Tunisia

Fatimid architecture

In the 10th to 12th centuries, an area including present-day Algeria, Tunisia, Sicily, Egypt and Syria came under the rule of the Fatimid dynasty who, through their dedication to building and design, triggered a renaissance in the decorative arts and the emergence of a common architectural vocabulary. Cairo (founded 969 CE), the 'City of a Thousand Minarets', became the cultural centre of the Islamic world.

Cairo's first big mosque was Al-Azhar, 'the splendid' (969–73, opposite). It features a hypostyle prayer hall with five aisles, a central courtyard and a stucco exterior showing influences from Abbasid, Coptic and Byzantine architecture. The huge mosque of Al-Hakim (c.996–1013) consists of an open courtyard surrounded by four halls. The mosques of Al-Aqmar (1125) and Al-Salih Tala'i (c.1160) are among the first examples of monumental small mosques, built to serve local needs but still with ornate detail. The Fatimids also developed elaborate tombs, such as those of the Mamluk sultans outside the walls of Cairo.

Romanesque

While Byzantine and Islamic architecture were flourishing, areas of western Europe that had once been part of the Roman Empire were in decline. It was not until Charlemagne (c.742–814 CE) was crowned Holy Roman Emperor in 800 that a significant new architectural style spread across Europe.

Charlemagne, determined to unite his empire and validate his reign, began building churches modelled after those of early Christian Rome. The resultant style was a fusion of Roman, Carolingian and Ottonian, Byzantine and Germanic traditions, with a generally massive and heavy quality. Romanesque churches were built on cruciform (cross-shaped) plans, with side aisles, galleries and a large tower over the nave and transept (central crossing point). Stone barrel or groin vaults supported the roofs, walls were thick, arches were usually semicircular and windows were both few and small. As the Romanesque spread across Italy, France, Germany, Scandinavia and England, it diversified into many local styles.

Church of Saint Nectaire,
France, c.1150

Italian Romanesque churches

Despite its Roman Italian origin, the Romanesque style south of the Alps followed its own unique path – in part because of the political autonomy of the Italian regions. Romanesque churches in Italy generally followed the plan of traditional basilicas (see page 70) but, in Lombardy in particular, they developed a more ambitious appearance. Colourful Tuscan marble, used widely in Pisa and Florence, created strikingly variegated exteriors, in contrast to Romanesque churches elsewhere. For instance, San Miniato al Monte (pictured), built in the 12th century in Florence, follows a classical and elegant style, with blind arcades and a patterned marble façade. The Baptistery of St Giovanni, built in Florence in 1059–1128, is octagonal and embellished with white and green marble. The classically influenced buildings in Pisa's Piazza del Duomo, begun in 1153, include the Baptistery, with its transitional Romanesque-Gothic style; the Duomo, or cathedral, sheathed in white banded marble and delicate arcades; and the famously leaning Campanile, or bell tower, also ringed with arcades.

Carolingian

The artistic revival inspired by the emperor Charlemagne later became known as the Carolingian Renaissance. While its architecture was a conscious attempt to emulate Roman achievements, it also borrowed heavily from early Christian and Byzantine styles and introduced new ideas of its own. Carolingian churches are generally basilican in shape, like the early Christian churches of Rome, and commonly incorporated the innovation of a westwork: a monumental west-facing entrance. The Palatine Chapel at Aachen or Aix-la-Chapelle (792–805 CE, opposite) is a fine example: inspired by the sixth-century octagonal Byzantine church of San Vitale in Ravenna, it also features a colossal westwork. Charlemagne commissioned the chapel along with his palace (which no longer stands), and drafted in builders from Italy. Based on an octagonal ring of arches, flanked by a circular gallery, the Palatine Chapel's east end had a square apse, and was originally flanked by two basilica structures. Its designer, Odo of Metz (742–814 CE), is the earliest-known architect born north of the Alps.

Ottonian

The Ottonian style of architecture evolved during the reign of Holy Roman Emperor Otto the Great (936–75 CE). Following on from Carolingian, it developed in Germany and lasted from the mid-10th until the mid-11th century. Like Carolingian, Ottonian contributed to the wider Romanesque style. Among other traits, it adopted the Carolingian double-ended variation on the Roman basilica, with apses at both ends of the nave rather than just one. Ottonian builders retained the huge Carolingian westworks and outer crypts, but the architecture was generally simpler, more systematic and monumental.

Saint Michael's in Hildesheim, Lower Saxony (founded c.1001) embodies the style, with two crypts, two apses and two transepts – each with a square crossing tower – in a geometric arrangement. The Ottonians also developed heavy columns and piers, wall arcades and blind arches around windows. Proportions were nevertheless simple and balanced, with careful attention paid to mathematical harmony.

Church of St Cyriakus, Frose, Germany, c.960

Vaults

Arched roofs of stone, or vaults, have been a fundamental element of architecture since early times. To create large open spaces, roofs had to span great distances, and for many early builders vaults were the only solution. In its simplest form a vault is an arch, and the simplest of all is the barrel vault (also called the waggon or tunnel vault), which is semicircular in section, like a cylinder cut in half lengthwise. Early examples of barrel vaulting go all the way back to the Sumerians, ancient Egyptians and, especially, the Romans. The Romans also used groin vaults, in which two barrel vaults cross at right angles, as at the transept of a church. (The groins are the arcs traced by the intersecting planes.) Romanesque developments enabled the joining of vaults of different spans and heights; but the great advance was the Gothic rib vault, in which the arcs evolved into raised ribs and load-bearing arches. Some rib vaulting became decorative and highly complex – such as sexpartite (six-panelled) vaults and fan vaulting – in the great Gothic churches and cathedrals built across medieval Europe.

Cluniac

During the 250 years after its foundation in 910 CE, the monastic house of Cluny (pictured) grew to be the most important in Europe. Thousands of monasteries and churches were built in its Romanesque style, spreading from Germany to France and often sited along popular 12th-century pilgrimages.

Among the most important of these was St Sernin in Toulouse (c.1080–1120), the largest church along the route to Santiago de Compostela in Spain. Built in a soft orange brick, on a crucifix plan, St Sernin has a long, barrel-vaulted nave with transverse arches and a 65-metre (213-ft) octagonal bell tower. The basilica is 115 metres (377 ft) long and 21 metres (69 ft) high, creating a vast, calm interior space. Nine chapels leading off the transepts and apse enabled pilgrims to pay their respects to relics, which in previous eras were usually hidden away from view in crypts. The Cathedral of Santiago de Compostela itself mirrors St Sernin: built in 1075–1122, mostly from granite, it too has nine radiating chapels and a wide ambulatory (processional walkway).

Castles

Medieval castles were built primarily as residences for the wealthy and powerful and their immediate communities, but they were also fortified strongholds and centres of administration. Defences included thick, high walls, secure entry gates, rock foundations and a moat, cylindrical towers, arrow loops and crenellations. To withstand sieges, an integral fresh water supply was vital.

After the fall of the Carolingian empire in the ninth and tenth centuries CE, castles spread across Europe and the Middle East. One of the world's finest surviving medieval castles is the 11th-century Krak des Chevaliers in Syria (opposite). Following William, Duke of Normandy's conquest of England in 1066, he used castles to assert control over the Anglo-Saxon people, who outnumbered the Norman aristocracy. Many were originally built from earth and timber, and were later rebuilt in stone. Between 1066 and 1087, William established 36 castles, including Dover Castle, the Tower of London and Windsor Castle.

Moorish Spain

The conquest of a large part of the Iberian peninsula by Islamic Moors from 711 CE brought a new concept of art and architecture into an area more familiar with Christian traditions. For the next eight centuries, mosques, castles and residences were built in a blend of Islamic and Christian styles, though this mixed tradition lasted longer in some places than others. For instance, the Christian recapture of Barcelona in 801 left little time for Moorish influence to establish itself, while the longer-lasting settlement of Aragón and eastern Castile left an extensive legacy including the 12th-century Aljafería Palace in Zaragoza. In Andalusia, where the Muslim presence extended over 800 years, Moorish buildings are even more prevalent. Under the rule of the Syrian prince Abd ar-Rahman (756–88 CE), Córdoba was transformed into a prosperous city. At its centre rose the Great Mosque (built from 785 and extended by subsequent rulers). Its giant, double-storey horseshoe arches of red and white stone (opposite) stand on 856 columns of jasper, onyx, marble and granite, forming 19 naves.

The Alhambra

The Red Fortress of Granada (*Qal' at al Hamra* in Arabic) was a mosque, palace and fortified complex, built in stone and timber for the last Muslim emirs in Spain and the Nasrid dynasty. Most of the surviving building was built between c.1333 and 1391 during the time of Muhammad V. Moorish poets described it as 'a pearl set in emeralds', alluding to the colour of its buildings and wooded environs. Built on a mountainous site, it did not follow a strict plan. Surrounded by horseshoe arches, the Court of Lions contains a fountain in an alabaster basin ringed by 12 white marble lions. Water flows from these to the four cardinal compass points. Evoking lightness and grace, the design expresses balance and symmetry, while decorations include geometric shapes, flowers and calligraphy. The Court of the Myrtles, with its long pool and finely columned arcades, leads to the Hall of the Ambassadors, or throne room, containing a vaulted wooden ceiling inlaid with seven tiers of interlacing star-shaped patterns – alluding to the seven heavens mentioned in the Qur'an.

Stave churches

Scandinavia remained outside the Christian sphere until about the middle of the 11th century, when Anglo-Saxon missionaries returned with Viking raiders from England and preached Christianity. The missionaries also brought knowledge of Christian church architecture with them, and soon began to put up small, simple churches based on a fusion of English Christian churches and native styles. These stave churches were usually wooden and windowless, the name deriving from the load-bearing posts in the timber framing, which were called *stafr* in Old Norse. Although they were once common across all of northern Europe, most surviving examples are in Norway, such as the church at Urnes, dating from *c*.1125 to 1140 (although it is possible that a previous Christian church was on the site). Bringing together elements of Celtic and Viking art and Romanesque architecture, the small, dark building (opposite) has cylindrical columns and semicircular arches with carvings and sculpture on many internal wooden panels, predominantly featuring interlaced Celtic-style patterns.

Gothic cathedrals

With their towers, flying buttresses and tracery (stone window framings), Gothic religious monuments were the supreme expression of Christianity in architecture. They represented a synthesis of God, humanity and nature, a blend of symbolism and efficient structures, and size became a dominant feature. From outside, the towers and pinnacles form intricate silhouettes against the sky as they soar towards Heaven; the vast, airy interiors, with hazy or coloured light pouring through the stained glass, seem similarly unearthly.

It was technical advances of the 12th century that elevated cathedrals from the heaviness of Romanesque to the lightness of the Gothic style. A major change was from thick to thin walls: the tonnage of roofs and towers was now transmitted to the ground not through stout walls but via a load-bearing 'skeleton' of pointed arches, ribbed vaults and multiple rib-like flying buttresses. Rain was shed from lead-covered roofs and spouted away from the walls through chutes or gargoyles.

Chartres Cathedral,
1194–1250

Saint-Denis and Chartres

The Gothic style in Europe originated in a new choir at the abbey of Saint-Denis near Paris, in 1140. Built under the direction of Abbot Suger (1081–1151), it revolutionized architecture. The unknown architect remodelled the church (opposite) with pointed arches, huge stained-glass windows, high stone vaults and flying buttresses. Previously, such lavishness was considered too garish and showy for a Christian building, but in his interpretation of the Bible, Suger saw his church as an image of God's kingdom. He ordered it to be flooded with coloured light, achieving an unprecedented brightness. Arches also pointed up to Heaven and allowed new types of vaulting.

This blend of spiritual vision and engineering skill spread to other churches. The first Gothic cathedral, Chartres (1194–1220), was built of limestone with a green copper roof. Dominated by flying buttresses and two contrasting spires, the cruciform plan features a spacious nave and façades bearing hundreds of sculpted figures depicting biblical themes.

Early Gothic

While the innovations at the choir of Saint-Denis spread quickly in Europe, some countries embraced them more readily than others. Germany was initially cautious. France was ambitious and enthusiastic, applying Gothic mainly to religious buildings. One of the first ribbed vaults after Saint-Denis was the nave of Saint-Étienne at Caen in the 1120s (although it was preceded by Durham Cathedral in England, opposite, in c.1090).

With the rediscovery of Euclidian geometry in the early 12th century, early Gothic cathedrals achieved a spatial unity and harmony, the style developing partly through a revival of mathematics and science and partly on time-honoured intuition. What constituted drawings and plans at that time became more accurate – as, consequently, did construction. Flying buttresses countered the outward thrust from the high ceiling and walls, and rounded arches gave way to lancet (pointed) arches, which held greater loads and also laid emphasis on a religious sense of Heaven-directed yearning.

French Gothic

Medieval communities took great pride in their churches and cathedrals, especially in northern France, source of the Gothic style. They poured huge funds into them, while professional masons travelled from city to city to build them. Sainte-Chapelle in Paris (1248, opposite) was designed to be more awe-inspiring than any other church in Europe. The resting place of holy relics, including a supposed piece of Christ's Crown of Thorns, it is an example of the Rayonnant style. A mid-Gothic phase inspired by French court style, Rayonnant – 'radiating' – is characterised by rose windows featuring decorative tracery. The walls of Sainte-Chapelle feature vast, brilliantly coloured stained-glass windows, separated only by vividly painted columns.

Close by, Notre Dame de Paris was begun in 1163; its flying buttresses were an afterthought, added to support the high, thin outside walls and roof. Over many years, numerous architects worked on Notre Dame; those of the mid-13th century oversaw the construction of the fine rose windows.

English Gothic

Gothic in Britain absorbed influences from other parts of Europe – as can be seen in its pointed arches, vaulted roofs, buttresses, large windows, tracery and spires – and yet its relative insularity resulted in a uniquely British synthesis. As they had done with the preceding Norman (Romanesque) style, masons and craftsmen introduced ideas from France to England, where Gothic was retrospectively divided into three periods: Early English (1200–75), Decorated (1275–1375) and Perpendicular (1375–1520).

An Early English example is the choir of Canterbury Cathedral (opposite), rebuilt in Gothic style after a fire in 1174. Salisbury Cathedral (1220–58) is also in the Early English style; the west front, although decorated, is flat and plain in comparison with its flamboyant French counterparts. Other Early English examples include Westminster Abbey, largely rebuilt in 1245 and 1269, and the late 12th-century Galilee chapel at Durham Cathedral, with slender columns supporting highly decorated arches.

Decorated and Perpendicular

Decorated architecture, also called Geometric, Middle Pointed or Curvilinear, has a lighter feel than Early English. It is characterized by ornately patterned windows divided by closely set mullions (vertical stone divisions), usually including trefoils and quatrefoils. The proliferation of flying buttresses saw interiors soar even higher, with slimmer columns, larger windows and greater decoration. Vaulting became lighter, with lierne (short-branch) or tierceron (full-length) 'spare ribs' making elaborate patterns, such as those at Lincoln, Exeter, Wells (opposite) and Bristol cathedrals; fan vaulting made its debut at Gloucester in the 1350s.

The chief characteristic of Perpendicular (or Rectilinear), England's final phase of Gothic, was an emphasis on vertical lines, most obviously in ranks of particularly close-set window mullions. Fan vaulting reached its zenith, too, with particularly fine examples at King's College Chapel, Cambridge (1446–1515) and Henry VII's Chapel at Westminster Abbey (1503–19).

Late Gothic

During the course of the 13th century the Gothic style grew more daring and coherent. Refinements to arches, vaults and buttresses permitted complex floor plans and huge cathedrals, with large, sculptural windows bearing elaborate tracery and fine stained glass. In France, after the collapse of Beauvais cathedral in 1284, with its ambitiously high nave – a record-breaking 48 metres (157 ft) – architects focused less on size, more on refinements in decoration. From the 14th century, Rayonnant gave way to the Flamboyant style, named after its extravagant, flame-shaped tracery. Pinnacles, mouldings and windows became more intricate, and columns slimmer. The abbey church of Saint-Denis was largely rebuilt, and Chartres cathedral and Notre Dame were given elaborate new façades. Beyond France, the high choir of Cologne cathedral (1248–1322, opposite) is one of the best German examples of Rayonnant, while Antwerp cathedral (consecrated 1521) is a late Gothic building with huge stained-glass clerestory windows; its single soaring tower was intended to have a twin, which was never completed.

Bastides

By the 13th and 14th centuries, experience had proved that walls punctuated by cylindrical towers were efficient for the defence of towns, cities and castles. In southwest France, several new fortified towns – *bastides* – were built, not only to protect residents but also to promote trade. Roughly following Roman town plans, bastides were built to strict grid layouts usually around a central square, with equal space allocated to each house. Not all were constructed to the same plan, but many shared certain characteristics, including a right-angled road layout of intersecting streets, wide thoroughfares, a church adjacent to the main square, and a market hall and *couverts* (covered arcades) close to the perimeter. People were offered incentives to settle in them and work on the surrounding land. Almost 700 bastides were built between 1222 and 1372, and while their architecture is not extraordinary, the plans are harmonious and became copied elsewhere. Bastide halls and churches were often originally constructed in wood, but later rebuilt in stone.

Cordes-sur-Ciel, Tarn,
southern France

Medieval secular architecture

Many new towns and cities were established in Europe during the high and late middle ages; from the 12th century on, the spread of urbanization saw the construction of town halls, guilds and other mercantile and civic buildings. In Britain, new towns sprang up around castles; Edward I created settlements to pacify the recently conquered principality of Wales, such as in Caernarfon and Conwy. Across Europe, the establishment of building regulations led to new rules on the heights and shapes of buildings, the widths of streets, projections of roofs, plus waste management, drainage and fire regulations. At Siena in Italy, for example, official regulations governing the dimensions of the palaces facing the Piazza del Campo date from 1298. Other extant cities that adhered to such structural rules were in Belgium, where some of the finest Gothic architecture appeared in town halls. Spain is home to some well-preserved Gothic castles; and in England, the university buildings of Oxford (opposite) and Cambridge are outstanding examples of Gothic civic architecture.

The Forbidden City

Commissioned by the Ming emperor Chang Zu (1360–1424), and built in 1406–20, the Forbidden City served as the Chinese Imperial Palace for nearly 500 years. The 980-building complex comprised audience halls, residences and courtyards on 7.2 hectares (18 acres) protected by a high wall and a moat, and entry was strictly by imperial permission. Not seeking to build lasting monuments, the Chinese constructed buildings reflecting the opposing forces of yin and yang, and they focused on the relationship of buildings to each other and to the landscape. Most buildings are made of wood, marble and specially baked bricks from Suzhou, with overhanging roofs supported on beams, posts and brackets. Laid out on a grid with a north–south axis, buildings were typically decorated with colourful glazed tiles and dragons, with yellow roofs symbolizing respect. Buildings include the halls of Supreme Harmony and Central Harmony, and palaces of Heavenly Purity and Earthly Tranquillity. Five marble bridges spanned the River of Golden Water that meanders through the city.

The Renaissance in Italy

That Italy should be the crucible of Renaissance architecture is no surprise: it was a short, if momentous leap for it to forsake Gothic and revive the ideals of ancient Rome, whose ruins were so close at hand. The Italian architects of the era felt a close affinity with art (many were, in fact, artists), and their vision focused more on form than on structure.

In 1452, architect and humanist Leon Battista Alberti published *De Re Aedificatoria* (*On the Art of Building*), after studying ancient Rome. Following *De Architectura* (*c.*15 BCE) by Vitruvius, Alberti's treatise covered history, town planning, engineering, sacred geometry, humanism and philosophies of beauty. The book was a revelation, setting out in mathematical detail the key elements of architecture – square, cube, circle and sphere – and ideal proportions. And as rich patrons in the city states vied to outdo each other with opulent palaces, it became part of an architect's essential training to study the relics of Rome, especially the Colosseum and the Pantheon.

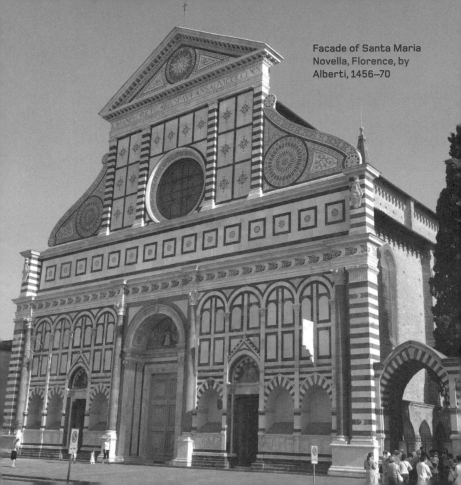

Facade of Santa Maria Novella, Florence, by Alberti, 1456–70

Florence

Italian Renaissance architects replicated many of the stylistic elements of ancient Rome, albeit with modern (i.e. post-Gothic) engineering skills, along with a humanist influence and ordered rationality. At Florence, one of the wealthiest cities, grand stone buildings included the Pazzi chapel (1441–78); the Palazzo Pitti, commissioned in 1458 by the Florentine banker Luca Pitti (1398–1472); the Palazzo Strozzi, built from 1489 for one of the city's richest families; and the Palazzo Medici Riccardi, designed by the architect and sculptor Michelozzo di Bartolomeo (1396–1472) and built in 1444–84 for Cosimo de' Medici, head of the banking dynasty. Massive, almost cube-like, Michelozzo's imposing construction for the Medicis combined classical elements – such as fine-grained sandstone, rusticated masonry, cornices and an open, central colonnaded court (opposite) – with new Renaissance concepts. Throught their highly individual interpretations of traditional elements, architects acquired an elevated status and a new artistic freedom of expression, and the new architectural ideas spread to other cities.

Filippo Brunelleschi

The Florentine Filippo Brunelleschi (1377–1446) is widely considered the first Renaissance architect, although his early works were still related to Gothic designs. Trained as a goldsmith in Florence, he travelled to Rome to study ancient buildings, and began working as an architect from that time. One of his greatest feats was the massive dome of Florence Cathedral, the Santa Maria del Fiore, or Duomo (c.1420–36). It was a remarkable feat of engineering incorporating not one, but two domes, one inside the other. He even had to invent special machines to hoist each section into place. The building's plain exterior includes a series of blind arches, while the interior is composed of flat surfaces and Doric, Ionic and Corinthian columns. With their apparent simplicity, Brunelleschi's designs evoke a sense of rationalism and proportion; for instance, his Hospital of the Innocents (1419, opposite) is based on a modular cube. The Basilica of San Lorenzo (1420–69) links elements of local building traditions with the architecture of ancient Rome.

Santa Maria del Fiore

Although this Florentine cathedral is predominantly Gothic in design, it is seen as a testament to the remarkable achievements of the Renaissance. Surmounted by Brunelleschi's magnificent ribbed dome, the patterned red, green and white marble exterior is the consequence of the city's efforts to eclipse its great rivals, particularly Siena and Pisa. In 1294, the city council commissioned architect Arnolfo di Cambio (1240–1310) 'to make a design ... in a style of magnificence which neither the industry, not the power of man can surpass'. Arnolfo designed the huge, vaulted basilica with an octagonal crossing, but it required a dome so enormous that it was beyond the scope of any contemporary architect. The cathedral's construction continued for over 100 years with various additions and adjustments, but the failure to build the dome remained a source of embarrassment for the Florentines. Then Brunelleschi won a competition and began building his 45-metre (148-ft) pointed dome c.1420, without scaffolding. It remains the largest masonry dome ever built.

Leon Battista Alberti

The Early Renaissance architect, humanist, writer, priest, artist, linguist and philosopher Leon Battista Alberti (1404–72) is recognized as a founder of modern architectural theory, asserting that the ideal design is a balance of form, function and decoration. In 1447, he became architectural advisor to Pope Nicholas V. His design for the façade of the Palazzo Rucellai in Florence (1451, opposite) included pilaster orderings with Doric, Ionic and Corinthian columns, rusticated masonry and a heavy cornice. His façade for the church of Santa Maria Novella (1458–71), also in Florence, features a geometric pattern of multicoloured marble and an entrance based on elements of the Pantheon in Rome, with columns, niches, pilasters and volutes. From 1450 to 1468, Alberti reconstructed the Tempio Malatestiano in Rimini, turning it from a Gothic church into a Renaissance mausoleum, and basing the façade on an ancient Roman triumphal arch. His 1471 design for the basilica of Sant'Andrea, also with a colossal triumphal arch, served as an important model for many later Renaissance churches.

Italian urban planning

During the Renaissance, Italy was a collection of city states, each with its own ruler – the Pope in Rome, the Medici family in Florence, the Doge in Venice, the Sforza family in Milan and the Este family in Ferrara. Through intense rivalry, technical and artistic developments increased, and new towns and cities were planned and constructed. Strict building regulations were set, endorsed by architects' guilds. The new nobility, created by wealth through banking or trade, commissioned imposing palaces, cathedrals, churches and town halls, while streets were arranged around large squares, created for markets and socializing. Brunelleschi's discovery of a new technique for drawing linear perspective led to the development of detailed architectural drawings, enabling projects to be easily visualized and shared. As printing developed, the dissemination of these ideas became easier, too. In 1484–5, Leonardo da Vinci planned his ideal city, basing it on a geometric plan and integrating elegant buildings, canals and roads on two levels.

The Ideal City (1480–4) by Fra Carnevale exemplifies
Italian Renaissance ideas about architecture.

Topkapi Palace

The main residence of the Ottoman sultans for almost 400 years, the Topkapi Palace in Istanbul was also the administrative, educational and artistic centre of the Ottoman Empire. Although it was mostly built during 1460–78, later sultans made their own alterations and additions, particularly Sultan Suleyman during the period 1520–60. The vast complex comprises low buildings constructed around courtyards and linked by galleries and passages. Trees, gardens and fountains in the courtyards create a sense of tranquillity. Seclusion was one of Suleyman's priorities, so special gates, courtyards and passages were built solely for his family's use. For instance, the massive Imperial Gate was his entrance into the first courtyard, a large open space surrounded by high walls that led on to three more courtyards. The fourth courtyard was a private area for the sultan and his family, while visitors to the palace entered through the Gate of Salutation and the second courtyard. The Tower of Justice symbolizes the sultan's watchfulness, and also served as his private lookout.

St Peter's Basilica

St Peter's in Rome stands on a site venerated since the first century CE as the burial place of Peter the Apostle. In 326, the emperor Constantine built an opulent church on the site which served for over 1,100 years. In the 16th century, Pope Julius II (1443–1513) commissioned from Donato Bramante a new church for the site and the adjacent Vatican Palace. The design was in a Greek cross format, with four small domes on each extension and a huge central dome, rising to a height of 136.5 metres (448 ft), raised on four huge piers. The construction would take 120 years (1506–1626) and undergo radical changes under a succession of designers. After Bramante died in 1514, Raphael (1483–1520) took over, succeeded after his death by Baldassare Peruzzi (1481–1536), then Antonio da Sangallo (1485–1546). After him, Michelangelo (1475–1564), at age 72, reluctantly took on the job, drawing the design into a cohesive unity that was largely preserved after his death by the final architect, Carlo Maderno (1556–1629), but for the late addition of a nave and a grand façade overlooking St Peter's Square.

Bramante

The initiator and leader of High Renaissance architecture was Donato Bramante (1444–1514), appointed chief architect in Rome when it replaced Florence as the artistic capital of Europe. After an intensive study of Roman ruins, Bramante created a new style of church, centrally planned, based on squares, circles and octagons, which expressed his ideals of geometry and harmony and incorporated elements of ancient pagan temples. Bramante's clarity of vision and fine sense of scale are expressed in the tiny, circular Tempietto at San Pietro in Rome (opposite), a Doric shrine built in 1502 on the traditional site of Saint Peter's martyrdom. The Tempietto is perceived as a High Renaissance masterpiece, fusing classical antiquity with new ideas. For instance, the slender Tuscan-style colonnade around the small cella (inner chamber) is topped by a semicircular dome on a tall drum, while the balustrade was new and inventive. Around the Doric entablature (the horizontal element over the columns), Bramante replaced pagan imagery with witty symbols of Christian liturgical instruments.

High Renaissance

Italian architecture during the late 15th century and early 16th saw still further refinements in the assimilation and translation of Roman ideas; buildings became less massive, as architects followed Bramante's lead in combining the ideas of Vitruvius, Alberti and Leonardo; meanwhile, the contrasting approaches of Raphael and Michelangelo ensured a diversity of styles prevailed during the High Renaissance.

The central plan arrangements of Roman temples became especially popular, with Francesco di Giorgio (1439–1502), Peruzzi, Raphael and Sangallo expressing these in churches, cathedrals, suburban villas and palaces, such as the Villa Farnesina (1505–10), the Villa Madama (1518–25) and the Palazzo Farnese (begun 1517, opposite), all in Rome. Michelangelo's New Sacristy in the Medici Chapels (1521–4) in Florence, and the Church of Santa Maria degli Angeli e dei Martiri (1563–6) in Rome, demonstrated classical interpretations fused with even more ambitious new ideas.

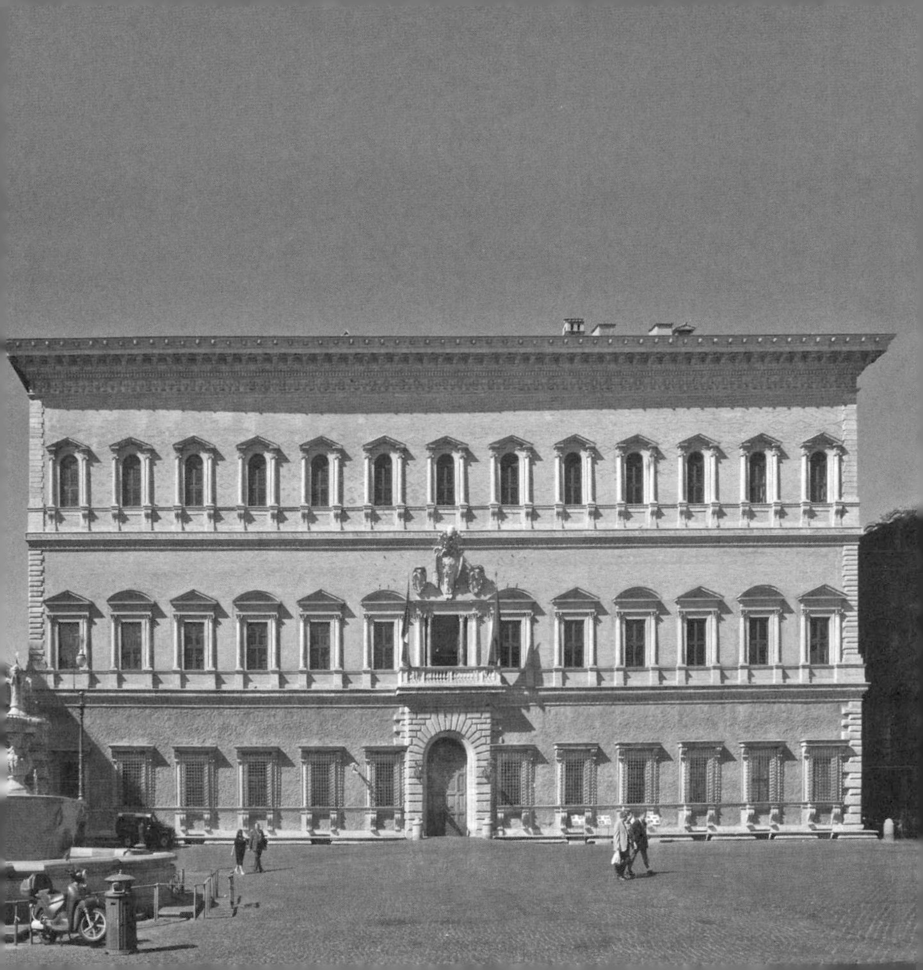

The Renaissance
beyond Italy

From Italy, largely through the advent of the printing press, the Renaissance slowly spread around Europe, emerging with varying interpretations. In northern Europe, France was the first country to absorb and translate the ideas. In the 1530s, architects Philibert de l'Orme (c.1510–70), Jean Bullant (1515–78) and Pierre Lescot (c.1510–78) visited Rome and took ideas back to France. L'Orme and Bullant worked on projects for the influential Queen of France Catherine de' Medici (1519–89), while Lescot took charge of building the Palais du Louvre for Francis I, turning it into a grand symmetrical palace from 1546. In England, Robert Smythson (1535–1614) built Hardwick Hall in Derbyshire (opposite). The Italian influence can be seen in the building's symmetry and classical-looking loggia, a double-storeyed open gallery above the front entrance. In Antwerp, the architect and sculptor Cornelis Floris (1514–75) was one of the many influenced by *L'Architettura*, published by Sebastiano Serlio (1475– c.1554) in 1537, and mixed Italian styles with Flemish traditional architecture.

French châteaux

Renaissance architectural interpretations in France emerged chiefly in the grand châteaux, built for royalty and the nobility. L'Orme and Bullant designed and rebuilt the Château de Chenonceau (opposite, 1514–22) in the Loire Valley with elaborate windows, chimneys and turrets, and an elegant five-arched bridge that reflects in the River Cher beneath. Inspired by a sketch by Leonardo da Vinci, the Tuscan architect Domenico da Cortona (c.1465–c.1549) designed and built the Château de Chambord (1519–47) for Francis I. Although it has many Gothic features, Chambord also expresses the Italian Renaissance in its symmetry and elaborate ornamentation. Built on a rectangular plan, it has enormous round towers at each corner, dormer windows, turrets, plus a main hall built to a Greek cross plan and an unusual double-helix openwork staircase. Architects Gilles le Breton (d.1553) and Sebastiano Serlio rebuilt the medieval Château de Fontainebleau (1528–47) for Francis I; the oval courtyard, private king's gallery, huge oval stairway and garden are key Renaissance additions.

Mannerism

Mannerism describes the approach of certain architects who pushed the limits of accepted Renaissance styles, often featuring exaggerated proportions and inventive blends of elements. For some Mannerists this approach came from an incomplete understanding of classical proportions; others knew them well but chose to override them. Michelangelo, one of the latter, became the best-known architect associated with the style. His Biblioteca Laurenziana (1524–71) in Florence, for instance, expressed his forceful, imaginative and revolutionary ideas about space and proportion. Similarly, his designs for St Peter's in Rome were inspired by, but contrasted with, the classical ideas favoured at the time.

Mannerism was not confined to Italy. The El Escorial Palace near Madrid, for instance, designed by Juan Bautista de Toledo (c.1515–67), who had worked on St Peter's, and completed in 1584 by his apprentice, Juan de Herrera (1530–97), is Mannerist in its simplicity and severity (opposite).

Palladio

The enduring fame of Andrea Palladio (1508–80) – who gave his name to an entire style – rests largely on the beautifully proportioned town and country villas he built for rich patrons in and around Venice. As a young man he visited Rome and absorbed the styles of antiquity, particularly the proportions of Greek and Roman temples; he later assimilated the style of the Mannerist Michele Sanmicheli (1484–1559). From his first designs around 1540, Palladio's signature elements became apparent, including paired flanking wings for stables and barns, walled courtyards and arcaded pavements, as well as impeccably symmetrical colonnaded façades. His designs did not call for expensive materials; stuccoed brickwork, hinting at Roman classicism, was a common feature. Published later in life, his *Four Books of Architecture* (1570), summarizing his studies of classical forms, gained him wide recognition, and his *Antiquities of Rome* (1554–6) was for 200 years the standard guidebook to the city. The timeless appeal of Palladian style would be eagerly taken up in 18th-century England.

Villa Foscari near Venice,
Palladio, 1558–60

Palladian style

Based on Palladio's designs and theories, the Palladian style found its greatest expression in Britain during the 17th and 18th centuries, peaking in fashion during the Georgian era, c.1715–60. With emphasis on clarity, order and symmetry, Palladianism asserted the primacy of reason and the principles of classical antiquity (leading, in the work of some later architects, to a rather sterile academic formula devoid of Palladio's own forcefulness and poetry).

Palladian buildings include churches, country houses, palaces and civic buildings, usually with plain, symmetrical exteriors and richly decorated interiors. Common elements include porticoes, grand staircases, rusticated ground floors, giant Corinthian columns supporting entablatures, semicircular arches, scallop shell motifs, and pediments over exterior doors and windows. The style was established in Britain by Inigo Jones (1573–1652), William Kent (1685–1748) and Richard Boyle (1694–1753), and its legacy is apparent in neoclassical and baroque architecture.

Chiswick House London,
William Kent, 1726–9

Inigo Jones

Inigo Jones was one of the greatest English architects of his era. After returning from travels in France and Italy (1613–14), he developed his own unique style from a blend of ancient, Renaissance and Palladian architecture. His plain, dignified designs for the Queen's House at Greenwich (1635) were based to some extent on the Medici villa at Poggio a Caiano, near Florence, but detailed in a style closer to Palladio or Vincenzo Scamozzi (1552–1616). The Queen's House, the severely classical Banqueting House in Whitehall (1619–22) and the Queen's Chapel at St James's Palace (1623) were radically different from the picturesque Jacobean style of the day. With their focus on symmetry and harmony, directly inspired by Palladio's *Four Books of Architecture*, Jones's designs sparked a revolution in English architecture. He was also in charge of the regulation of new buildings in London; his Covent Garden (1630), an open space surrounded by arcaded houses and a church (opposite, dubbed 'the handsomest barn in England'), effectively introduced formal town planning to the capital.

Domes

The Roman development of concrete made it possible to build large, hemispherical domes. These became a major feature of Byzantine churches, especially once builders began using pendentives or squinches (corner supports) to mount them on rectangular buildings. Because of their comparatively shallow shape, Roman domes are sometimes described as 'saucer' domes. Islamic architects often created pointed or bulbous domes – such as on the Taj Mahal at Agra, India – which can be compared to the onion-shaped dome used in Russia, Germany and eastern Europe. In Italy, both Brunelleschi and Michelangelo designed double-shelled domes that were hemispherical internally, but slightly pointed externally to direct the weight more downward than outward; both the inner and outer domes rest on a circular drum, which is often set with windows. St Paul's Cathedral in London is a triple-shelled dome. Compound domes are groups of multiple domes on one building, as seen on, for instance, St Basil's in Moscow. Generally, domes are crowned with a lantern or cupola.

Interior dome of
St Peter's Basilica, Rome

St Basil's Cathedral

Built in 1555–61 on Moscow's main marketplace by the order of Ivan IV the Terrible (1530–84), the Cathedral of Vasily the Blessed – St Basil – was a symbol of the might of Russia and its tsars, commemorating Russian victory over the Mongols at Kazan in 1552. The architect is not known, though the names Barma and Posnik are cited. The colourful variegated onion domes have become a symbol of Moscow, and of Russia as a whole, though they are in fact 17th-century replacements for the original helmet-shaped domes

Although the building looks asymmetrical from the outside, the interior follows a formally structured plan, with the main church in the centre and eight chapels arranged evenly around it. Each side chapel has its own distinctive tower, surmounted by a dome, and is connected to the others by narrow winding passages. While the style of the church appears unique, some elements resemble those in the wooden churches built in northern Russia in previous eras.

Humayun's tomb

The first example of Mughal architecture in India was the Tomb of Humayun (1508–56), the second Mughal emperor. Built in Delhi, it was commissioned by his widow, Bega Begum (1511-82), who was also buried there. Designed and built by the Persian architect Mirak Mirza Ghiyas, it was also the first Mughal structure to use red sandstone on such a scale. Construction began in 1566 and continued under the reign of Humayun's son, Akbar the Great (1542–1605).

White marble was used for cladding, flooring, lattice screens (*jaalis*), door frames, eaves (*chhajja*), and for the double-shelled main dome, which stands 47 metres (154 ft) high and 91 metres (299 ft) wide. Set on a high, square platform, the tomb is the focal point of a garden divided formally into four quarters, each of which is then subdivided into nine. This quartered garden is a Persian representation of paradise, with flat surfaces separated by ornamental streams, paved pathways and avenues of trees. Humayun's tomb directly inspired the design of the Taj Mahal.

Blue Mosque

The Blue Mosque in Istanbul is arguably the last great mosque of the classical period of Ottoman architecture (1437–1703). Its correct name is the Sultan Ahmed Mosque, but the popular title comes from the blue paint and 21,043 Iznik tiles, which cast an atmospheric glow. Designed by Sedefkar Mehmed Agha (c.1540–1617) on the site of the former Roman hippodrome, the mosque amalgamates some Byzantine elements of the neighbouring Hagia Sophia with traditions of Islamic architecture. With one main dome, six minarets and eight secondary domes, the Blue Mosque is surrounded on three sides by a marble courtyard, which includes an imperial lodge, double-height shops and a theological college. The main dome is 43 metres (141 ft) high and 23.5 metres (77 ft) in diameter. The interior is illuminated by over 260 stained-glass windows and hundreds of oil lamps hung from the ceilings. The Iznik ceramic wall tiles are decorated with flowers, fruit and cypresses, marble paving covers the floors, and the *mihrab* (a niche indicating the direction of Mecca) is also of fine marble.

Taj Mahal

Expanding on design traditions of both Persian and Mughal architecture, the Taj Mahal near Agra was inspired by love and grief and took over 20,000 workers 22 years to build. In 1631, the fifth Mughal emperor Shah Jahan (1592–1666) ordered the mausoleum to be built for his late wife, Mumtaz Mahal (1593–1631), who had died giving birth to their 14th child. Wanting the mausoleum to be more beautiful than anything ever built, he rejected red sandstone as its main fabric, which had become the primary Mughal building material, and chose instead white marble, decorated with inlay work of semi-precious and coloured stones. The Persian chief architect, Ustad Ahmad Lahauri, designed it to be perfectly symmetrical: a square building in the centre of a marble plinth almost 6 metres (20 ft) high and 96 metres (315 ft) square, with a huge double-constructed central dome. The inner dome is 24 metres (79 ft) high, and the central octagonal structure beneath it is surrounded by a two-levelled passageway with an octagonal tower at each corner. A raised rectangular pool reflects the building serenely.

Baroque

The first truly international movement in architecture and art, the baroque style originated in the early 17th century in Rome, then spread across Italy and to Spain, France, Germany and Britain, and later to Scandinavia, Russia and parts of South America, lasting until the mid-18th century. Extending ideas of the Renaissance, the style manifested in different ways in different countries. As part of the Counter-Reformation, it was a singular attempt by the Catholic Church to strengthen its image, show its power and make a strong emotional and sensory appeal to the faithful through art and architecture. Characterized by sweeping curves, complex plans, *trompe l'oeil*, drama, grandeur and dramatic effects of light and shade, the style also features highly decorated interiors and rich surface treatments that blur the lines between architecture and art. Many baroque buildings feature bright colours and vividly painted ceilings. The word comes from the Portuguese *barocco*, meaning misshapen pearl, and was applied to the movement retrospectively.

Church of St Nicholas,
Prague, 1703–52

Bernini, Borromini and da Cortona

Prominent baroque architects included Gian Lorenzo Bernini (1598–1680), Francesco Borromini (1599–1667) and Pietro da Cortona (1596/7–1669). Early on, they worked together on the Palazzo Barberini, which had been started by the architect Carlo Maderno, but they became fierce rivals. Bernini was also the greatest sculptor of the baroque, as well as a painter and poet; his sculpture and buildings epitomize the flamboyance, theatricality and splendour of the period. Among many prestigious commissions were his contributions to St Peter's in Rome: the large piazza in front of the basilica, an immense gilt-bronze baldachin (canopy) over St Peter's tomb inside, and the decoration of the four huge piers supporting the dome, plus grand statues. Borromini, originally a mason, challenged tradition with audacious combinations of elements and proportions. Cortona's church of Santi Luca e Martina (opposite, 1634) was one of the first curved façades in baroque Rome, with closely packed composite orders, while his Santa Maria della Pace has an unexpected, temple-like semi-oval portico.

Venice

Venice's architecture developed as a fusion of Italian, Byzantine and Islamic ideas. Sculptor and architect Jacopo d'Antonio Sansovino (1486–1570) introduced High Renaissance architecture there, particularly in his Biblioteca Marciana (1537–60) and mint (1537–45), facing the Doge's Palace (opposite). Palladio declared that the library, with its 21-bay arcade and barrel-vaulted staircase, was the finest building erected since antiquity. Scamozzi extended Sansovino's library and completed Palladio's San Giorgio Maggiore and Teatrico Olimpico after their deaths. His treatise *The Idea of a Universal Architecture,* along with buildings such as the Palazzo Contarini (1609–16), provide a link between the High Renaissance and the baroque. Baldassare Longhena (1598–1682), who trained with Scamozzi, completed his Procuratie Nuove in St Mark's Square. His Santa Maria della Salute shows the influence of Palladian classicism, while its huge dome is anchored by massive baroque scrolls to an octagonal base, and his Ca' Pesaro (begun 1659) exemplifies the Venetian baroque.

François Mansart and Jules Hardouin-Mansart

Henry IV's entry into Paris in 1594 as king of France heralded a period of political and social aspiration. Architecture reflected this, with the bourgeoisie commissioning country houses – *châteaux* – and town mansions, or *hôtels*. By the mid-17th century, the baroque style had found expression in the form of palaces, first in France with the Château de Maisons (opposite, 1651) near Paris, built by François Mansart (1598–1666), and later across Europe. Most of Mansart's patrons were those who had prospered in the service of the crown. His buildings are elegant and harmonious, as can be seen in his Château de Blois (1635–8); his extensive use of a four-sided, double-slope roof, with dormer windows, lent its name to the mansard roof.

Adopting his grand-uncle and teacher's surname, Jules Hardouin-Mansart (1646–1708) served as Louis XIV's chief architect. He enlarged the royal château of Saint-Germain-en-Laye, and from 1675 added extensions to Versailles, including the Grand Trianon, the Orangerie and the fifth chapel.

Versailles

Starting life as an extension of Louis XIII's hunting lodge in 1623, the Palace of Versailles was built for Louis XIV, the 'Sun King', from 1668 to 1710. The main architects were Louis le Vau (1612–70) and Hardouin-Mansart, whose many collaborators included landscape architect André Le Nôtre (1613–1700) and painter Charles Le Brun (1619–90). Versailles grew into one of the world's largest palaces, the summit of French baroque, embodying the absolutism of the monarchy. Standing more than 400 metres (1,300 ft) long, the palace takes the form of a grand central block and two flanking wings set around a central courtyard. The complex includes five chapels, the Grand Trianon (1687–8), the Pavilion Français (1749) and the Petit Trianon (1762–8). The Hall of Mirrors (Galerie des Glaces), the palace's glittering central gallery, is one of the most famous rooms in the world. The palace, its decoration and extensive grounds stimulated a rebirth of decorative art. From 1682 to 1789, approximately 3,000 people, including the king and the entire French royal court, lived at Versailles.

Melk Abbey

Towering over the River Danube in Lower Austria, Melk Abbey was commissioned by the abbot Berthold Dietmayr (1670–1739). It follows the designs of Jakob Prandtauer (c.1660–1726), and was completed in 1736 after his death by his nephew, Joseph Munggenast (1680–1741). The Benedictine abbey, church and monastery is the largest in Austria and Germany, standing as a bastion of Catholicism and exemplifying the spirited approach to the baroque taken by its country's architects. On the site of a previous 11th-century abbey, the imposing ochre-and-white stuccoed building features a grand dome topped by an exotic lantern, with a curved façade emphasized by two onion-domed bell towers. Planned around a central axis 320 metres (1,050ft) in length, the main building is flanked by outbuildings, including the huge marble abbey hall and a double-storey library. Elaborately painted ceilings, gilded decoration and sculpture feature throughout, created by Johann Michael Rottmayr (1656–1730), Paul Troger (1698–1762), Lorenzo Mattielli (1687–1748) and Peter Widerin (1684–1760).

Christopher Wren

Although best known as an architect, Sir Christopher Wren (1632–1723) was also an expert in anatomy, astronomy, mathematics, geometry, mechanics, biology and optics. After founding the Royal Society and reading Vitruvius, he took an interest in architecture and in 1665 visited Bernini in Paris. At the time, the profession of architect did not formally exist, and it was not unusual for well-educated gentlemen to take it up as a branch of mathematics. His first project was the chapel of Pembroke College in Cambridge, commissioned by his uncle, the bishop of Ely, in 1663, but he is remembered best for St Paul's Cathedral (1674–1710). He had been involved in repairing the old cathedral since 1661, and in 1666 he designed a dome for it – but within a week, the Great Fire destroyed the building along with most of London. So Wren designed a new cathedral, along with the entire City of London, including several new churches. Wren also built the Sheldonian Theatre in Oxford (1663), the Royal Hospital at Greenwich (opposite, 1696–1742), and the Wren Library at Trinity College, Cambridge (1676–84).

Hawksmoor

Nicholas Hawksmoor (1661–1736) was a leading architect of the English Baroque, along with Wren and Vanbrugh. He helped design some of the finest buildings of the period, including St Paul's Cathedral and Hampton Court Palace, but also made his own singular contributions.

Raised in Nottinghamshire, Hawksmoor became clerk to Wren at age 18. From c.1700, he helped Vanbrugh at Castle Howard (where he designed the Mausoleum, opposite) and Blenheim Palace. He designed London churches, including Christ Church, Spitalfields and St George's in Bloomsbury, its pyramidal steeple a clue to his unusual taste for pagan symbols. He also designed university colleges – notably in the heart of Oxford, where he added a Gothic flavour to All Soul's College (1716–35) to integrate it with the adjacent medieval buildings, and conceived the Clarendon Building (1711–15) in the neoclassical style. One of his last commissions was for Westminster Abbey, where he designed the great towers flanking the western front.

Vanbrugh

Architect, soldier, playwright and politician John Vanbrugh (1664–1726) was, with Hawksmoor, the leading exponent of the English Baroque style, demonstrating it abundantly in two colossal palaces. The first, Castle Howard in Yorkshire (opposite, 1702–12), won him instant acclaim as well as his next commission, Blenheim Palace in Oxfordshire (1705–22). He later designed Seaton Delaval, Northumberland (1718–28).

Though still untrained when he took on Castle Howard, Vanbrugh had an inherent grasp of architecture, particularly in creating a sense of grandeur and drama, and many of his buildings incorporate elements from castles, such as battlements and towers. He also blended medieval and classical forms with traditional English ideas. It is possible that he was influenced by the French Baroque style while imprisoned in France for espionage (1688–93). All his buildings were collaborations with Hawksmoor, who provided the practicality that Vanbrugh needed to realize his ambitious designs.

St Paul's Cathedral

Until the late 20th century, St Paul's Cathedral was the tallest building on London's City skyline, designed by its architect, Sir Christopher Wren, to tower over the spires of his other city churches. Its location on Ludgate Hill has been a site of worship for over 1,400 years. Wren's cathedral, completed in 1708, replaced Old St Paul's, destroyed by the Great Fire of 1666. A synthesis of medieval, Gothic, classical and baroque styles, its commanding feature is the dome rising 111 metres (365 ft) to the spire at its summit. Built on a Latin cross plan, St Paul's has a classical portico at each end. Wren was familiar with the unique octagonal lantern tower of Ely Cathedral (where his uncle was bishop), which spans the aisles as well as the central nave. He adapted this for St Paul's dome, which is raised on a tall drum surrounded by pilasters and pierced with windows in groups of three, separated by gilded niches. Echoing St Peter's Basilica in Rome, the dome is double-shelled, with a load-bearing brick core. The west front is based on the eastern façade of the Louvre, designed by Claude Perrault (1613–88).

Johann Neumann

Johann Balthasar Neumann (1687–1753) was a late baroque architect working mainly in the towns of Würzburg and Bamberg in Bavaria. His original style amalgamated Austrian, Bohemian, Italian and French elements, creating commanding and well-balanced buildings, and he introduced the new rococo style to his interiors.

Neumann's work was exceptionally precise yet light-hearted, playful and colourful, with none of the heaviness of some baroque architecture. He used symmetry and harmony to create astonishing visual effects, mainly for churches and palaces such as the Würzburg Residenz (1720–44, opposite). Domes and barrel vaults enhance the illusion of elegance, while light streams through huge windows onto lavish ornamentation, murals and gilding. His Wallfahrtskirche or 'pilgrim's church' (1730–9) in the town of Gossweinstein was a colossal sandstone building with two high towers facing the town. His final work, the Marienkirche at Limbach (1747–52), is a masterpiece of the baroque style.

Rococo

Emerging from the gilded splendour of the Palace of Versailles (1623–82), the rococo developed as a lavish, decorative style in contrast with the baroque preceding it. The name derives from the French word *rocaille*, which described the shell-covered rock-work used to decorate artificial grottoes, and *coquille*, meaning seashell. Rococo architecture is light-hearted and frivolous, with abundant curves, scrolls, gilding, elements of fantasy and ornament. Where the drama of the baroque emphasized balance and stability, rococo was graceful and fluid, and accentuated asymmetry. Outstanding examples include the Catherine Palace in St Petersburg (1717–23), designed by Johann-Friedrich Braunstein, the Queluz National Palace in Portugal (1747–92), designed by Mateus Vicente de Oliveira (1706–86), and the Chinese House in Potsdam, Germany (1738), designed by Emmanuel Héré de Corny (1705–63). Other notable rococo architects include Francesco Bartolomeo Rastrelli (1700–71), Philip de Lange (c.1705–66) and Matthäus Daniel Pöppelmann (1662–1736).

Church of Saint Francis of Assisi, Ouro Preto, Brazi, 1766

The Wieskirche

One of the most famous works of rococo architecture, the Wieskirche in Steingaden, Germany, was built in 1745–54 to house a dilapidated wooden statue of the Scourged Christ that in 1738 had been seen by several locals to shed real tears. As pilgrims arrived from all over Europe to see the miraculous statue, the local abbot decided to commission a special shrine. Local artists and architects Dominikus Zimmerman (1685–1766) and his brother Johann Baptist (1680–1758), designed a confection of a building, chiefly white and gold, and filled with elaborately curving and gilded stucco and colourful paintings. The church is oval in plan, with columns in front of the walls supporting a cut-out cornice and wooden vaulting. To the east, a long, deep choir is surrounded by an upper and lower gallery. Dominikus, in charge of the project, ensured that all the elements worked together – so for instance, the building harmonizes with the surrounding landscape, and the *trompe-l'œil* ceiling paintings appear as an iridescent blue sky with flying angels, contributing to the atmosphere of exuberance.

Neoclassicism

The shift in thinking known as the Enlightenment marked a period of intellectual, social and political zeal that began in France in the early 18th century and rapidly spread abroad. Developments in printing had increased literacy among the middle classes, and ideas developed in nearly every aspect of life, including education, economics, law, science and social and political reform. The key terms for the age became order, balance and harmony, and once again the virtues of ancient Greece and Rome were seen as the height of discernment. Neoclassicism was also inspired by discoveries in the 18th century of two ancient Roman cities beneath volcanic ash from the eruption of Mount Vesuvius in 79 CE. It signalled a return to order and rationality after the theatrical baroque and the frivolous rococo (although its earliest traces were apparent in baroque buildings, such as St Paul's Cathedral). Neoclassical architecture is characterized by grandeur of scale, simplicity and geometric forms, Greek or Roman detail, dramatic use of columns and a preference for plain white walls.

Vilnius Roman Catholic
Cathedral, Lithuania (1769–83)

Parisian Neoclassicism

Neoclassicism had surfaced in architectural design late in Louis XVI's reign, emerging more fully during the first Napoleonic Empire as architects experimented with a range of civic buildings. It had begun with the Church of Saint Genevieve – or the Panthéon – in Paris (1756–97), designed by Jacques-Germain Soufflot (1713–80), which combines the purity and magnificence of Greek architecture with the lightness and daring of Gothic construction. This unorthodox interpretation of classical forms became even bolder leading up to the French Revolution, with the Royal Saltworks at Arc-et-Senans (1775–8), designed by Claude-Nicolas Ledoux (1736–1806), and the Arc de Triomphe (1806–36), by Jean Chalgrin (1739–1811). The Place de la Concorde, an octagon spanning 359 x 212 metres (1,176 x 696 ft), bordered by the River Seine to the south and neoclassical buildings to the north, was designed by Ange-Jacques Gabriel (1698–1782) in 1755; Pierre-Alexandre Vignon (1763–1828) designed the Church of the Madeleine (c.1842, opposite), a monumental temple-like building with Corinthian columns.

Neoclassicism in Britain, Germany and Russia

In newly industrialized Britain, architects such as John Nash (1752–1835) and John Wood the Younger (1728–82) reshaped London and Bath with neoclassical streets, crescents and parks. Sir John Soane (1753–1837) designed the Bank of England (1792); and Sir Robert Smirke (1780–1867) created the British Museum (begun 1823). Robert Adam (1728–92) designed country houses in his own detailed and unique interpretation of the classical style.

German neoclassicism was inspired by the writings of Johann Winckelmann (1717–68) and supported by Friedrich Wilhelm II of Prussia. It emerged through architects such as Karl Friedrich Schinkel (1781–1841), who designed Berlin's many-columned Altes Museum (1823–30), and Carl Gotthard Langhans (1732–1808), whose Brandenburg Gate (1793) was based on the Propylaea of the Acropolis. In Russia, meanwhile, Catherine the Great commissioned Charles Cameron (1745–1812) to design the Pavlovsk Palace (opposite, 1782–6), and Giacomo Quarenghi (1744–1817) to plan the Alexander Palace (1812).

Neoclassicism in the USA

By the late 18th century in the United States, ancient Greek and Roman architectural styles had become very popular as they were expressive of the young nation's democratic ideals. The Capitol, with its neoclassical façade and dome, is attributed to William Thornton (1759–1828), Benjamin Latrobe (1764–1820) and Charles Bulfinch (1863–44), and was begun in 1793, following Thornton's plan. Inspired by the Louvre and the Panthéon in Paris, the building is centred on a grand entrance (opposite), framed with projecting wings and accentuated by vertical columns. Initially timber, the dome and rotunda were later rebuilt in stone and cast iron. The third US president, Thomas Jefferson (1743–1826), drew upon Palladian and classical ideals in his designs for the Virginia State Capitol (1788), the Rotunda at the University of Virginia (1822–6), and Monticello House (1768–1809). The White House in Washington DC was designed by James Hoban (1758–1800), following his Charleston County Courthouse (1790–2); Jefferson and Latrobe added the east and west colonnades, for laundry and stables, in the 1900s.

Beaux-Arts

France had been one of the first countries to create a formal system of architectural training with the founding of the Académie Royale d'Architecture in 1671. Although the academy was closed during the French Revolution, its function was revived in the École des Beaux-Arts, which Napoleon opened in 1803. Developed from the teachings at the new school, Beaux-Arts – 'fine arts' – architecture is an ornate classical style that spread rapidly, emerging in public buildings around the world.

Beaux-Arts architecture focused on symmetrical plans and drew inspiration from classical styles. It often features slightly oversized details, high rusticated basements, deep cornices, and recessed arches and pediments that are commonly adorned with reliefs. The Paris Opéra (1860–75, opposite), designed by Charles Garnier (1825–98), and the Petit Palais (1896–1900) by Charles Girault (1851–1932) – both students of the École des Beaux-Arts – embody the style.

The Industrial Revolution

European architecture in the 19th century was profoundly altered by the Industrial Revolution of *c.*1760–1840. In earlier times, for instance, multi-storey buildings depended on stout walls and buttresses: the taller the building, the thicker the lower sections had to be. That changed when forged iron and milled steel began to displace wood, brick and stone as primary materials for the infrastructure of tall buildings.

As machinery took over menial tasks, towns expanded as workers moved from farms to factories. Buildings sprang up to meet demand, including town halls, museums, libraries, hospitals, shops, schools, colleges, banks, offices, warehouses and factories. The advent of rail travel – the first passenger railway was opened in England in 1825 – created a need for new structures, such as stations, railway hotels and bridges. Technological progress inspired architects with new ideas, but they also borrowed from diverse historical styles, including Greek, Roman, Islamic, Byzantine, Gothic and Renaissance.

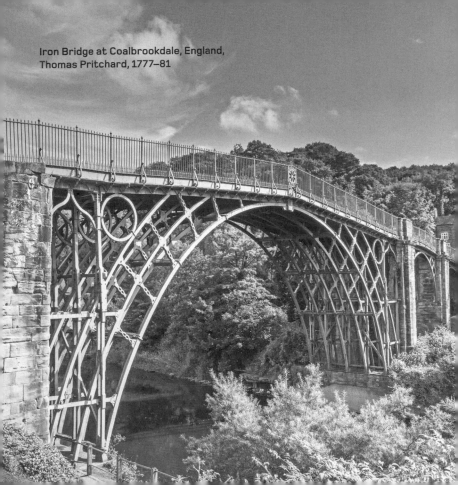

Iron Bridge at Coalbrookdale, England,
Thomas Pritchard, 1777–81

Joseph Paxton and Gustave Eiffel

Improved production of cast iron and steel enabled 19th-century architects to build on a new and massive scale, and advances in sheet-glass manufacture led to a vogue for conservatories and greenhouses. In 1837, gardener Joseph Paxton (1803–65) built the largest conservatory in the world for his employer the Duke of Devonshire. He later built the vast, prefabricated Crystal Palace in Hyde Park, London, for the Great Exhibition (1851). Covering some 92,000 square metres (990,000 sq ft), the cast-iron, timber and glass structure (opposite) had no precedents. It took eight months to build and even less time to dismantle.

In 1889, French civil engineer and architect Gustave Eiffel (1832–1923) built a tower in Paris as the centrepiece of the Universal Exposition. Designed with an open lattice to minimize wind resistance, it comprised 18,038 separate components, all made in Eiffel's factory on the city's outskirts and assembled on site. Until the construction of New York's Chrysler Building (1930), the Eiffel Tower was the world's tallest structure.

Railways

The myriad advances of the 19th century altered lives beyond all recognition; arguably the greatest change was created by railways. By the 1840s, railways reached all parts of England and many other parts of Europe and elsewhere; in 1869, the first transcontinental line linked the east and west coasts of the United States. Railways had become the wonder of the age, and distinctive styles of architecture developed around them. Philip Hardwick (1792–1870), Robert Stephenson (1803–59) and Charles Fox (1810–74) created Euston Station in London in 1837, with its propylaeum (grand gateway) and Doric columns. A determination to outshine the neoclassical King's Cross Station (1851–2) and Great Northern Hotel (1854), designed by Lewis Cubitt (1799–1883), spurred George Gilbert Scott's (1811–78) design for St Pancras Station and Midland Grand Hotel (opposite, 1865–76). Convinced that the Gothic style was the only true Christian style, Scott gave these buildings castellated fringes, dormer windows, towering pointed roofs, banded 'neo-Byzantine' arches and Venetian-inspired façades.

Gothic Revival

Following the Renaissance, the Gothic style had been ridiculed and generally considered ugly, thanks in no small part to painter and architect Giorgio Vasari (1511–74). He had labelled medieval architecture 'Gothic,' declaring that the Goths had invented it after sacking Rome. But by the 1830s, several architects were re-evaluating church architecture: they saw Gothic as truly Christian, and dismissed classicism and neoclassicism as 'pagan'. Devout Catholic Augustus Welby Northmore Pugin (1812–52) argued that a return to the medieval styles of architecture would lead to the revival of a morally upright Christian society. John Ruskin (1819–1900), a leading art critic and patron, draughtsman, watercolourist and philanthropist, wrote *The Seven Lamps of Architecture* (1849) and *The Stones of Venice* (1851–3), promoting the virtues of a Protestant form of Gothic architecture. The third significant theorist of the Gothic Revival was the French architect Eugène Emmanuel Viollet-le-Duc, who had become known for his restorations of medieval buildings.

Budapest Parliament Building,
Imre Steindl, 1885–1904

Palace of Westminster

London's old Houses of Parliament, which burned down in 1834, dated back to the 12th century, and the fire provided an opportunity to replace them with a modern structure suitable for governing Britain. In 1833, noted architect Charles Barry (1795–1860) won a competition to create the new building. During construction, he came to rely heavily on Pugin; while Barry favoured classicism, Pugin added many Gothic stylings. The façade of sand-coloured Yorkshire limestone stretches along the Thames for 289 metres (914 ft), and the vast building incorporates grand assembly chambers as well as committee rooms, kitchens, offices and libraries. The building is dominated by two towers: the huge Victoria Tower and the soaring Clock Tower, known as Big Ben after the great bell inside it. The decorative Clock Tower, finials and turrets were largely designed by Pugin, who added ogees (double curves) and carved crockets (leaf-like elements bordering spires and roofs). Pugin was also in charge of the Gothic-styled interiors, and supplied designs for furnishings.

Tower Bridge

In 1877, a public competition was held to design a new bridge over the River Thames in East London. The challenge was to still allow tall-masted ships to reach the busy anchorages at the commercial heart of the British Empire. The winning architect, selected in 1884, was Sir Horace Jones (1819–87), who as well as being surveyor of the City of London also happened to be one of the judges. After his death his assistant George D. Stevenson took over, changing Jones's original brick façade to a more ornate Gothic style. Engineer John Wolfe Barry (1836–1918), son of Sir Charles Barry (see page 230) devised the idea of a suspension bridge with two massive concrete towers on piers sunk into the riverbed. The central span comprised a pair of bascules (balanced drawbridges) that could be raised to allow river traffic to pass; upper walkways served foot traffic and, more importantly, braced the towers against the horizontal force exerted by the bascules. The steel frame was clad in Cornish granite and Portland stone. Construction began in 1887, employing more than 400 workers for eight years.

Victorian Gothic

In Britain, the Gothic Revival reached its full flowering through Victorian buildings of the mid-19th century, but its roots were considerably older. Horace Walpole, 4th earl of Orford (1717–97), art historian and politician, had been one of the first to revive the Gothic style. Starting in 1749, he spent nearly 30 years building the fanciful, heavily adorned Strawberry Hill House in Middlesex (opposite). Other early British champions of Gothic included Robert Adam's rival, James Wyatt (1746–1813); his design for Ashridge Park in Hertfordshire, begun in 1806, features a huge central hall that imitates a medieval great hall. After an apprenticeship with Gilbert Scott, George Edmund Street (1824–81) became a leading practitioner of the Victorian Gothic Revival, known especially as the designer of the Royal Courts of Justice in London. Street made more than 3,000 drawings of his design, and construction took 11 years from 1873. The massive white building is reminiscent of French 13th-century cathedrals and châteaux, dominated by soaring pitched roofs, pointed arches, towers and half-towers.

Gothic Revival – Europe and America

Initially, the Gothic Revival was an English style, but by the second half of the 19th century it was appearing erratically in other parts of Europe and America. In 1879, Heinrich von Ferstel (1828–83) built the Votifkirche in Vienna, a national shrine to the Emperor Franz Joseph I (opposite). A unique interpretation of the 13th-century French Gothic style, it features two slender, soaring towers and lozenge-patterned tiling on the steeply pitched roof. Across the Atlantic, Richard Upjohn (1802–78) built Trinity Church in New York (1846), which features towering pointed arches, an 86-metre (281-ft) spire and jewel-bright stained-glass windows. Also in New York, the Woolworth Building on Broadway was designed by Cass Gilbert (1859–1934), with a modern steel skeleton and a strongly Gothic façade. Dominated by a massive central tower, the Woolworth Building (completed 1913) comprises 30 storeys, incorporating turrets, towers and lanterns with a copper-clad pitched roof. Because of its resemblance to European Gothic cathedrals, it was nicknamed 'The Cathedral of Commerce'.

Viollet-le-Duc

Through his restorations and descriptions of medieval buildings, Eugène Emmanuel Viollet-le-Duc (1814–79) inspired the Gothic Revival in France. Eschewing the neoclassicism of the École des Beaux-Arts, he studied French and Italian medieval architecture, and his first restoration for the Ministry of Historical Monuments was Saint-Germain-l'Auxerrois (1838) in Paris. The following year he oversaw the restoration of the abbey church of the Madeleine at Vézelay. With Jean-Baptiste-Antoine Lassus (1807–57), he worked on Sainte-Chapelle and Notre-Dame in Paris, which they restored in an overtly Gothic style. Yet although his renovations reproduced past ideas, they were blended with his unique Gothic sensibilities, which took them beyond restoration into the realm of invention. Nonetheless, in his *Analytical Dictionary of French Architecture from the XIth to the XVIth Century* (1854–68) and his *Discourses on Architecture* (1863–72), Viollet-le-Duc dominated 19th-century theories of architectural restoration, and would exert a powerful influence on modern design.

Château de Pierrefonds,
*c.*1400, restored by
Viollet-le-Duc 1857–85

Neuschwanstein Castle

High on a crag in southwest Bavaria stands the fairy-tale castle of Neuschwanstein. It was built c.1869–81 for King Ludwig II (1845–86) along the lines of two ancient castles: Wartburg in Germany and Pierrefonds in France, both constructed in the medieval style with massive walls, tall towers and battlements, and palatial interiors. Eduard Riedel (1813–85) designed Neuschwanstein in a Romanesque revival style then popular in Germany, featuring round-topped arches, barrel vaults and strong walls. Built of brick faced with limestone, the main towers have overhanging battlements with machicolations and carved masonry. The image of an ideal castle is, however, idealistic: there are no real fortifications. Inside, the turreted residential block is called the Knights' House, but no knights lived there. Instead, it housed offices and service rooms. Based on Hagia Sophia in Istanbul, the throne room includes rows of arches and an apse, with pillars of imitation porphyry and lapis lazuli. Neuschwanstein was the inspiration for the castle in Disney's *The Sleeping Beauty*.

Scottish Baronial

Alongside the classical and Gothic revivals of the 19th century, Scotland saw its own independent revival. Adopting elements of fortified local tower houses of the 16th century, and blended with medieval, Gothic and Renaissance components, Scottish Baronial style appealed to national pride. It was also inspired by the historical novels of Sir Walter Scott (1771–1832) and his house at Abbotsford, built in 1824 in the Scottish borders, with stepped gables and projecting turrets. When Queen Victoria acquired Balmoral as a holiday home and had it rebuilt in 1852–6, the crenellations, lancet windows and turrets of Balmoral became common features of the Scottish Baronial style, along with rough-hewn stone, gables and steep roofs. First emerging in rural areas, the style spread to cities, where townhouses adopted elements of the revival, such as crow-stepped gables, small windows and tiny bartizans (turrets) added to façades. The most prominent Scottish Baronial architects were William Burn (1789–1870), his pupil David Bryce (1803–76) and also Bryce's pupil, Charles G.H. Kinnear (1830–94).

Torosay Castle, Isle of Mull,
David Bryce, 1858

Arts and Crafts

Spurred by a reaction against industrialization, 19th-century English reformers created a new movement, instigated by designer, artist, writer and manufacturer William Morris (1834–96). Arts and Crafts gathered momentum and spread across Europe and the United States. In the belief that machines and mass-production were lowering the quality of life, proponents revived ancient crafts, collaborating in medieval-style workshops to hand-produce furniture, books, ornaments, tiles and other objects. Although these smaller items were the main concern, architecture had a prominent role. During an apprenticeship with the architect G.E. Street, Morris befriended Philip Webb (1831–1915), who became a leading Arts and Crafts architect and designer. A key tenet was 'truth to materials': materials were usually locally sourced, and functions of buildings determined their design and construction, with no excessive ornament. Many Arts and Crafts buildings recalled Tudor or Elizabethan manors, or Gothic styling, such as Webb and Morris's Red House (opposite, 1859) in Bexleyheath, Kent.

Orientalism

In the late 18th and 19th centuries, a fascination with 'the Orient' developed in the West. Although Eastern architecture was little understood by Western architects, many of its decorative stylings were adopted as exotic elements. In the 17th century, Dutch traders had brought Chinese mother-of-pearl, lacquer, silks and porcelain to Europe, and this led to a fashion during the rococo period for chinoiserie (a decorative style featuring Chinese motifs) and to increased imports of Chinese porcelain. In his book *Upon the Gardens of Epicurus* (1658), Sir William Temple (1628–99) used the term 'sharawaggi', from the Japanese *shara'aji*, meaning 'symbolism in design', to describe a pleasing irregularity in landscape design or town planning. In 1757, Frederick the Great of Prussia (1712–86) had a 'Chinese teahouse' built in the grounds of his palace in Potsdam, featuring palm-tree-shaped columns, a curving roof and statues of Chinese figures (opposite). The publication of architectural pattern books, such as *Rural Architecture in the Chinese Taste* (1750–2) by William Halfpenny, fuelled the fashion further.

The Royal Pavilion

In the 1780s, England's Prince George rented a lodging house in Brighton, then a fishing village. He hired architect Henry Holland (1745–1806) to extend the house into a modest villa and, fascinated by Eastern designs, furnished and decorated it lavishly with imported Chinese furniture and wallpapers.

In 1815, by now Prince Regent, George commissioned John Nash to rebuild his villa and convert it into a magnificent Oriental-style palace. With William Porden (c.1755–1822) and Humphry Repton (1752–1818) working on aspects of it, it became an eclectic blend of Indian and Chinese influences, although Nash remained the chief architect. By 1821, the building was complete, with picturesque turban domes, minarets, moulded plaster and copper palm-leaf decorations. The domes were covered in sheet iron and the sumptuous hall was based on an illustration of one at Allahabad in India. In 1820, Frederick Crace (1779–1859) and Robert Jones (dates unknown) were employed to create the exotic Chinese-style interior decoration.

Haussmann's Paris

In 1853, Emperor Napoleon III (1808–73) made lawyer Georges-Eugène Haussmann (1809–91) Prefect of the Seine Department, and he began renovating the unhealthy, congested streets of Paris. In 1850, most of the city was still as it was in the medieval period, with narrow, winding streets and open sewers, but its population had doubled since 1800 to over one million. The severe overcrowding bred disease and unrest, and the streets were confusing and congested. Haussmann demolished slums and designed a new, airy, open city of gaslit streets. Although he had no previous experience as an architect or an urban planner, he hired tens of thousands of workers to improve the city's sanitation, water supply and traffic circulation, and build wide avenues, parks and squares, sewers, fountains and aqueducts. Paris was divided into *arrondissements* (municipal districts), and many of the straight, wide boulevards intentionally created vistas of monuments or monumental buildings, such as the Arc de Triomphe and the Opéra, while buildings also had new, uniform façades.

Regency, Empire and Federal styles

Despite the advent of new movements in the 19th century, such as Arts and Crafts and Orientalism, neoclassicism endured as a popular architectural style. In Britain, where it was characterized by elegance and simplicity, it became known as the Regency style after George, Prince Regent from 1811–20, who commissioned John Nash to lay out some of the best-known areas of central London. Regency coincides with the Biedermeier style (1815–48) in German-speaking lands. In France, neoclassicism became known as Empire style, taking its name from Napoleon I's Empire of 1800 to 1815, and following his orders to uphold the standards of Republican Rome. (A neoclassical aesthetic had also pervaded France's Directoire style of the 1790s.) Charles Percier (1764–1838) and Pierre Fontaine (1762–1853) were prominent architects of the Empire style. The Empire and Georgian styles strongly influenced the Federal style that emerged in the United States between c.1780 and 1830, often called 'Adam style' after the Scottish brothers Robert (1728–92) and James (1732–94) Adam.

Brunswick Terrace, Brighton, built in the Regency Style around 1825.

Charles Garnier and Henri Labrouste

Charles Garnier (1925–98) studied in Rome in 1848 and absorbed the Byzantine style of Turkey and Greece. He also studied with the neoclassical architect L.H. Lebas (1782–1867) and worked briefly with Viollet-le-Duc. Garnier mixed industrial structural materials with flamboyant but controlled décor to produce such glamorous buildings as the Paris Opéra and the Monte-Carlo Casino in Monaco (opposite), which epitomize the Second Empire under Napoleon III (1852–70).

Henri Labrouste (1801–75) was a leading architect of 19th-century France. On leaving the École des Beaux-Arts, he spent six years in Rome (1825–30). One of the first architects to use iron-frame construction, he also believed that architecture should reflect society. His Bibliothèque Sainte-Geneviève in Paris (1843–50) sensitively exposes iron structural elements of columns and arches, while his reading room of the Bibliothèque Nationale (1860–7) comprises nine decorated metal domes supported by slim cast-iron columns.

Baroque Revival

By the late 19th century, students of architecture flocked to the École des Beaux-Arts from all over the world. The first American to attend was Richard Morris Hunt (1827–95), who helped found the American Institute of Architects in 1857. One of his many designs was the façade and Great Hall of the Metropolitan Museum of Art (opposite, opened in 1902) and the pedestal of the Statue of Liberty (1882–4). His grand mansions became identified with America's Gilded Age and demonstrate what became variously known as the baroque revival, neo-baroque, Imperial style or, in France, Second Empire architecture (and in Britain, Edwardian baroque). In France, the baroque was an essential part of architects' learning at the École des Beaux-Arts, and aspects of the style emerged in buildings around Europe. These include: City Hall in Belfast (1898–1906), designed by Alfred Brumwell Thomas (1866–1948); the Reichstag (Parliament) Building in Berlin (1889–98), designed by Paul Wallot (1841–1912); and the Piccadilly Hotel in London (1905–8), designed by Norman Shaw (1831–1912).

Art Nouveau

Spanning the quarter-century from 1890 until the outbreak of war, art nouveau was arguably the first avant-garde architectural style, and it manifested in all areas of design, from architecture to the fine and decorative arts. Art nouveau architects rejected revivalism and historicism, and instead embraced a completely new aesthetic that featured asymmetry, flowing lines, whiplash curves, organic forms, symbolism and new materials such as iron and glass. Architectural interpretations include the Hôtel Tassel (completed in 1893) in Belgium, designed by Victor Horta (1861–1947), designs for entrances to the Paris Métro (1899–1905) by Hector Guimard, the Secession House in Vienna (1896) by Joseph Maria Olbrich (1867–1908), the Glasgow School of Art (1897–1909) in Scotland by Charles Rennie Mackintosh, and La Sagrada Familia (begun 1882) in Spain, designed by Antoni Gaudí. Art nouveau came under a range of names, from *Jugendstil* (Germany) to *stile floreale* or *stile liberte* (Italy) and *modernismo* (Spain).

Majolikahaus in Vienna,
Wagner, 1898

Victor Horta and Hector Guimard

The townhouse Hôtel Tassel in Brussels was the first building conceived fully in the art nouveau style. Rather than hide structural elements, Belgian Victor Horta (1861–1947) used them as decoration; cast iron, for instance, appears in the form of plant-like tendrils snaking through the building. Horta was influenced by Viollet-le-Duc's maxim that machine-made materials be used to create 'architectural forms adapted to our time'. He exploited iron's load-bearing strength to make wide spans, maximising internal space as well as daylight.

Hector Guimard (1867–1942) designed his Métro entrances to coincide with the 1900 Universal Exposition in Paris. Built in iron, glass and green steel, they are filled with light, and stress organic, asymmetrical, delicate decoration. Such was their impact, art nouveau in France was sometimes called *Guimard style* or *style Métro* – even though they were criticized at the time. His own Paris home, Hôtel Guimard (1912), stands on a triangular plot and features curved walls and flowing forms.

Hotel Tassel in
Brussels,
Horta, 1893

Antoni Gaudí

The unique style of Catalan architect Antoni Gaudí (1852–1926) blends art nouveau and modernism with myriad other elements and influences, including Catalan and Moorish traditions, the Gothic revival and his own devout Catholic beliefs. His fluid lines and asymmetrical shapes convey a focus on natural motifs, with textured and undulating forms that recall the sea, coral, fish, dragons and lizards, as well as sinuous curves designed to glitter in the sun as the day passes. Structures such as Casa Mila (1906–10), Casa Batlló (1904, opposite) and Parc Güell (established 1914) feature unusual tracery, few straight lines, irregularly shaped windows and façades made of *trencardís*: a mosaic of colourful ceramic tile pieces. Casa Batlló's roof, for instance, resembles the back of a dragon, with balcony balustrades shaped like eye masks, and 'scales' of glistening *trencardís*; Parc Güell features colourful mosaic surfaces and a Doric colonnade. Gaudí's approach to architecture was always sculptural, with a perpetual dynamism deriving from his endlessly curving lines.

La Sagrada Familia

In his unfinished basilica of La Sagrada Familia (begun 1882), Gaudí replaced Gothic buttresses with slanted columns and added soaring pinnacles, expressive sculpture and dramatic façades. The spires, steeples and entrance portals, built on a massive scale, evince both Gothic and Spanish baroque styling. One of the few conventions he adhered to was the Latin cross format, but little else complies with tradition. Three façades illustrate scenes from the Bible – the Nativity, the Passion and the Glory, with sculptures of holy figures modelled from ordinary citizens of Barcelona – while towers represent the Evangelists and the Apostles. Multicoloured mosaics and 'pompom' finishes on some pinnacles symbolize the mitre, ring and staff of Catholic bishops. Although he followed a mathematical structure for the building, Gaudí drew few plans, working more with models and his own impromptu ideas. During his lifetime, Gaudí completed only 4 of the 18 towers he had planned. Nonetheless, La Sagrada Familia presents a unique, unified and astonishing interpretation of art nouveau.

Charles Rennie Mackintosh

Scots designer Charles Rennie Mackintosh (1868–1928) mixed art nouveau with Scottish Baronial ideas, the interlacing of Celtic art and design and the elegant simplicity of Japanese forms. He applied his unique linear style of right angles and ornate curves to all aspects of building and interior design. Between 1896 and 1906 he undertook major commissions for private homes, commercial buildings, interior renovations and churches, notably the Glasgow School of Art, of which the central and eastern parts were constructed first, and the second phase eight years later. Overall, the building appears to fuse medieval fortifications with industrial architecture and light, airy art nouveau elements. The Hill House in Helensburgh (opposite, 1902–3) is an extraordinary mixture of art nouveau, Arts and Crafts, Scottish Baronial and Japanese styles. In keeping with the art nouveau style, and all Mackintosh's buildings, the house is asymmetrical: roofs pitch and rise at different angles and heights, chimneys and turrets add to the irregular exterior, while the building itself evolved its shape from the interior plan.

Vienna Secession

Art nouveau in Austria and Germany was sometimes called *Sezessionstil* (Secession style) after the Vienna Secession, a group of painters, sculptors and architects who opposed the conservatism of the Künstlerhaus (home to the Association of Austrian Artists), and who took inspiration instead from the linear style of Mackintosh. In 1897, led by Gustav Klimt (1862–1918), they broke away from the Künstlerhaus and formed their own group. They put on exhibitions and produced a magazine, *Ver Sacrum* (Sacred Spring), extolling their beliefs and aims.

Architects in the group were Otto Wagner, Josef Hoffmann (1870–1956) and Joseph Maria Olbrich. Mixing industrial materials with ornamentation, Secession architecture was often strongly rectilinear, based on clean and simple geometric forms with decorated façades, commonly featuring curving lines and shapes (Horta's whiplash or 'eel' line was popular). Wagner, the eldest of the group's architects, declared: 'Nothing that is not practical can be beautiful.'

Karlsplatz Station in Vienna,
Wagner, 1899

Otto Wagner and
Joseph Maria Olbrich

Wagner (1841–1918), who served as Professor of Architecture at the Vienna Academy of Fine Arts, was initially a proponent of neoclassicism, later adopting more modernist ideas. From 1894 to 1910, he designed bridges and stations for the Stadtbahn (Viennese subway system). His restrained, geometric entrance to the Karlsplatz Station was a steel frame with marble slabs in the Stadtbahn colours of green, gold and white. Wagner also created the Austrian Postal Savings Bank, using aluminium, glass and marble in an airy and elegant structure.

Wagner's student Joseph Maria Olbrich (1867–1908) became the leading architect of the Vienna Secession and was chosen to design the group's exhibition hall (opposite, 1897). Loosely following the rectilinear style of Mackintosh, the hall is bold and simple, comprising large white rectilinear forms topped by a golden metal cupola of floral openwork. The building won much acclaim, and Olbrich was commissioned to help design the Darmstadt Artists' Colony in Hesse, Germany in 1899–1901.

Modernism

Modernism emerged in both Europe and the United States at the beginning of the 20th century, although neither the timing nor the term is definitive. Since the late 19th century there had been numerous attempts to assimilate modern technology into a new architectural style to embrace the new century, with skyscrapers – one of modernism's icons – appearing in the United States as early as the 1880s.

More a philosophy than a style, modernism in architecture emerged from an analytical approach that allowed the function of a building to dictate its form. Modernism rejected historical precedent and ornament, and favoured the rational use of 'new' materials, including steel, aluminium and concrete, often with large expanses of glass. The First World War interrupted most new developments, and although a few modernist buildings appeared before 1914, the movement really only gathered momentum after 1918. Overall, modernism wrought a profound transformation upon architecture.

Garden cities

In 1898, British reformer Ebenezer Howard (1850–1928) described a utopian city where citizens would live in harmony with nature (illustrated opposite). Out of this emerged the garden city movement: a method of urban planning that focused on organizing new towns, surrounded by countryside, that would give the working classes a healthy alternative to overcrowded inner cities. Howard's vision was for people to live in concentrically planned towns, with boulevards radiating from the centre, parks and open spaces interspersing built areas, and a generous garden for every dwelling. Once each city filled (to a maximum of 32,000 people), another would be built, leading to clusters throughout the country, linked by road and rail. With its roots in the Arts and Crafts movement, the garden city ideal incorporated all that a community would need. During 1903–07, Letchworth Garden City was built in Hertfordshire, followed by Welwyn Garden City, approximately 19 kilometres (12 miles) away, in 1920. The idea was influential in the United States, leading to the creation of cities such as Sunnyside in Queens (1924–8).

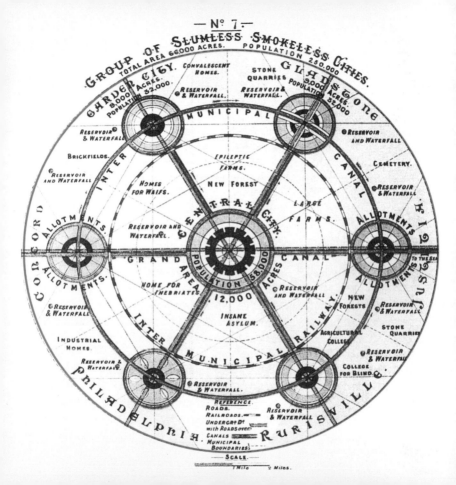

Skyscrapers

More than any other structure, the first skyscrapers of the late 19th century showed how site, purpose and materials exerted control over a building's design. Until this time, towers and church steeples had relied of necessity on thick or buttressed load-bearing walls: the liberation of tall buildings came through a mix of factors including a high premium on urban land, the use of steel in structural frameworks, and the evolution of the modern elevator. (Steam-driven safety elevators arrived in the 1850s, followed by electric models from 1902.)

The first major opportunity to exploit these new technologies came in the city of Chicago, largely rebuilt in the decades following the fire of 1871. William Le Baron Jenney's (1832–1907) ten-storey Home Insurance Building (opposite, 1884–5) was the first tall building to use fireproof steel as its framework, launching a revolution that would transform Chicago's skyline and, with it, modern architecture. As skyscrapers grew taller, tiered designs were developed to ensure light and fresh air reached street level.

Louis Sullivan

Known as the Father of American Modernism, Louis Sullivan (1856–1924), with his partner Dankmar Adler (1844–1900), embraced developing technologies to form a new language for tall buildings. In 1889, they designed the ten-storey Chicago Auditorium Building. As Chicago sits on a swamp, Adler devised a raft of timbers, steel and iron I-beams to 'float' the building on the marsh. In 1894 they developed a caisson construction for the Chicago Stock Exchange, which allowed water to be pumped out from the foundations. It became a model for tall buildings across the US. Decoration was not entirely omitted: in their 10-storey Wainwright Building in St Louis (1891), the steel-frame construction terminates in a frieze and projecting cornice, and their 16-storey Guaranty (now Prudential) Building in Buffalo (1896, opposite) is encased in terracotta. But while traces of neoclassicism, Romanesque revival, Romanticism and art nouveau show in his work, Sullivan was original. His Carson Pirie Scott department store in Chicago (1899–1904) also emphasizes verticality, but with large, horizontal windows.

Chicago School

The term 'Chicago School' came to describe the succession of architects, from William Le Baron Jenney on, who rebuilt the city after the great fire of 1871 and won Chicago its reputation as the birthplace of modern architecture. The Chicago School included William Holabird (1854–1923), Martin Roche (1853–1927), Daniel Hudson Burnham (1846–1912), John Wellborn Root (1850–91) and Adler and Sullivan, who were among the first to apply new technologies, particularly steel-frame construction in commercial buildings (the term 'commercial style' was widely used at the time).

The Chicago School was not a conscious or coherent group; there were no established principles to which they all adhered, nor did any of them produce a sole defining style of building. But all their buildings were individual and unique, utilizing numerous inventive construction techniques and materials. These pioneers are collectively known as the First Chicago School, with a Second Chicago School following the Second World War.

Marquette Building in Detroit,
Holabird & Roche, 1905

Form follows function

In 1896, in his essay 'The Tall Office Building Artistically Considered', Louis Sullivan asserted that 'form ever follows function, and this is the law'. He saw this 'law' applying as much to architecture as it did to the form of a bird, or a tree, or the human body. From then on, 'Form follows function' became a guiding principle of modernism. Although Sullivan did not claim to have coined the phrase, his timing was apt, and he became recognized for its widespread adoption from the turn of the 20th century. He attributed the idea to the Vitruvian virtues of *firmitas, utilitas et venustas* (see page 54) – that a building should be sturdy, useful and beautiful.

Modernism now meant designing from the inside out, in an inversion of traditional architectural principles, so that the purpose of a building should dictate its form. And although Sullivan himself often used ornament – for instance, in his organic and interlacing friezes inspired by art nouveau – decorative elements were firmly subordinated to function.

Functionalism

'Form follows function' generated the modernist approach of functionalism, even though functionalism can be argued to have been around since ancient times. It dictates that the form of a building be determined by its purpose, materials and structure, rather than by the aesthetic principles of an architect's designs. The rise of functionalism was spurred in part by rapid social and economic growth in America, which called for larger buildings. The new mass-production of steel led to skyscrapers with lightweight skeletons on which the rest of the building's elements – including, significantly, walls – were suspended. This column-and-frame construction allowed taller buildings with larger windows, which created lighter interiors. Many functionalist buildings were based on the three-part composition of a classical column: base, shaft and cornice. Successful functionalist buildings include the glass and steel AEG turbine factory in Berlin (1907–10), designed by Peter Behrens and New York's triangular 22-storey Flatiron Building (1902, opposite), by Daniel Hudson Burnham.

World fairs

The success of the Great Exhibition in 1851 in London inspired other countries to follow suit, promoting national successes and displaying their latest developments in science, technology and the arts. From mid-century on, major world fairs took place in several US cities and across the capitals of Europe. Fairs gave architects opportunities to present a nation's idealized version of the future. Chicago's Century of Progress fair (1933), for instance, included the steel-framed House of Tomorrow, designed by George Keck (1895–1980) to include an aircraft hangar as well as a garage; and the Armco-Ferro House, whose revolutionary prefabricated construction was designed for mass production. On a larger scale, examples of iconic structures from world fairs include Gustave Eiffel's eponymous tower (1889), and the Grand Palais in Paris (1900), designed by a team of four architects. Ludwig Mies van der Rohe (1886–1969), designed the German Pavilion for the 1929 exposition in Barcelona; despite extravagant materials, its simple form led to it becoming regarded as an important modernist building.

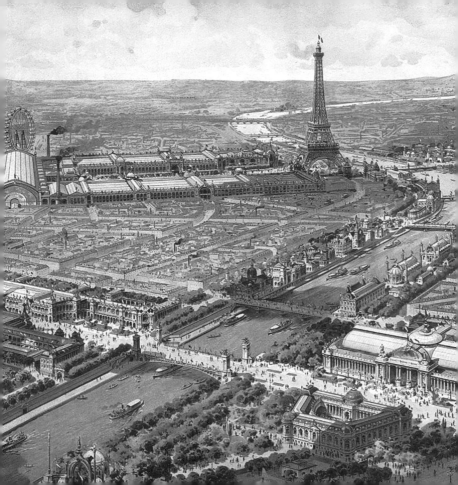

Frank Lloyd Wright

Structures designed in harmony with modern life and the environment were the hallmark of US architect Frank Lloyd Wright (1867–1959), who also designed his own furniture, fittings and stained glass. After studying engineering, Wright worked with Joseph Lyman Silsbee (1848–1913) and was apprenticed to Louis Sullivan. On leaving Sullivan in 1893, he designed the Winslow House in Illinois, with a strong horizontal emphasis and expansive interior spaces. Winslow House heralded a succession of Wright designs that, in their harmony with the environment and use of local natural elements, were later dubbed 'organic architecture'. His original approach and ideas emerged in offices, churches, schools, skyscrapers, hotels and museums; but designs like Winslow House, which exaggerated horizontals and low, pitched roofs, became known as the Prairie School of architecture. Many of his works defy categorization, such as the ochre concrete Fallingwater (1935, opposite), cantilevered above a Pennsylvania waterfall, and the white concrete spiral of the Guggenheim Museum (1959) in New York.

Prairie Houses

Inspired by Frank Lloyd Wright's article 'A Home in a Prairie Town,' published in a 1901 *Ladies' Home Journal*, the term Prairie Houses or Prairie School has been applied to a certain style of dwelling mainly built in midwestern America during the late 19th and early 20th centuries. Architects include Wright himself, Walter Burley Griffin (1876–1937) and George W. Maher (1864–1926).

Solid in construction, Prairie Houses emphasize horizontal lines, with single storeys, low-pitched roofs and overhanging eaves, long bands of casement windows, central chimneys, open-plan interiors and minimal ornamentation. Made mainly with local materials, they integrate well with the landscape; timber is unstained and unpainted, and other materials are left as natural as possible. Although they never used the term 'Prairie House' themselves, the architects all believed that horizontal lines evoked and related to the native prairie landscape. Wright's most acclaimed 'Prairie School' buildings include the Robie House in Chicago (1909) and and Laura R. Gale House in Oak Park (opposite, 1908).

Organic architecture

With parallels to the Arts and Crafts movement, Frank Lloyd Wright promoted a philosophy of architecture advocating harmony and unity between buildings and the natural world. In an article for *Architectural Record* in 1914 he stated that 'the ideal of an organic architecture . . . is a sentient, rational building . . . individually fashioned to serve its particular purpose'. And in his 1954 book *The Natural House*, he wrote: 'So here I stand before you . . . declaring organic architecture to be the modern ideal.' The concept of an organic style was not unique to Wright, and other architects had their own ideas about it, but he became its best-known proponent. It included the assertion that a site should be enhanced by a building, which should derive its form partly from the nature of the site. The relationship to the site should be unique, such that it would be out of place elsewhere. In natural settings, buildings might open out, and in urban places, turn in. Buildings were to grow out of the landscape as naturally as any plant, while materials should be used simply in ways that enhance and endorse their intrinsic character.

Solomon R. Guggenhem Museum
in New York, Wright, 1943–59

Less is more

Ludwig Mies van der Rohe, remembered as one of the 20th century's greatest architects, is also associated with the phrase 'less is more'. He was not, however, the first to use it; credit for that goes to Peter Behrens, who employed young Mies to collaborate on the AEG turbine factory in Berlin (1907–10). According to Mies: 'I heard it in Behrens's office for the first time. I had to make a drawing for a façade for a factory . . . I showed him a bunch of drawings of what could be done and then he said, "Less is more," but he meant it in another way than I use it.' Mies used the phrase often, effectively making it his own, as he reduced and distilled buildings and their components into simple, integrated forms. Like several other contemporary architects, he sought to create a new architectural style to exemplify modern times, and his focus on simplified components and minimal ornamentation led to designs featuring multifaceted buildings of glass, steel and glazed curtain walls that blurred the boundaries between interiors and exteriors.

330 North Wabash in Chicago,
Van der Rohe, 1969–73

Adolf Loos

Austrian–Czech architect Adolf Loos (1870–1933) was an influential theorist of modern design. After a conventional training and a three-year visit to the United States, he gave a lecture in Vienna in 1910 on 'Ornament and Crime', in which he attacked decoration in art, architecture and product design. His reputation grew with an essay in the magazine *Cahiers d'Aujourd'hui* in 1913: 'The evolution of culture marches with the elimination of ornament from useful objects,' he wrote, explaining that ornamentation – which he labelled 'immoral' and 'degenerate' – can effectively date buildings and objects. In its place, he advocated smooth and clear surfaces, free of the lavish decorations of art nouveau and the Vienna Secession. 'Freedom from ornament is a sign of spiritual strength,' he asserted. Loos's uncompromising and austere buildings, such as the plain-faced Goldman & Salatsch Building in Vienna (opposite, 1910) – then derided by the staid Viennese as 'the house without eyebrows', but now acknowledged as a landmark in *Wiener Moderne* – reflected his pioneering approach.

Peter Behrens and the Deutscher Werkbund

Widely regarded as the first industrial designer, and one of the most important architects of his time, Peter Behrens (1868–1940) was an influence on Mies van der Rohe, Le Corbusier, Walter Gropius and Adolf Meyer (1881–1929). A pioneer of corporate design for AEG (Germany's general electric company), he designed not only the factory and offices, but also the industrial products, stationery and company logo.

In 1907, seeking greater efficiency in the production of crafts, better design for industry and a more modern approach to architecture, Behrens helped establish the Deutscher Werkbund (German Work Federation), at the proposal of architect Hermann Muthesius (1861–1927). A state-sponsored fusion of art and industry, the Werkbund was indebted to the ideas of William Morris, as members (who included Gropius and Mies) sought to improve the design of everyday objects. Its motto was *Vom Sofakissen zum Stadtebau* ('from sofa cushions to urban construction').

Futurism

The rationale of futurist architecture, an Italian movement of the early 20th century, is best represented in hundreds of drawings by the architects Antonio Sant'Elia (1888–1916) and Mario Chiattone (1891–1957). Futurism's founder, the poet Filippo Tommaso Marinetti (1876–1944), produced its first manifesto in 1909. Inspired by the machine age and the glorification of war, futurists rejected the past in favour of radical new ideas, embodied in vast cities with soaring towers and megastructures. In 1914, Sant'Elia wrote the official *Manifesto of Futurist Architecture*, explaining how architecture should be meaningful and refined, and inspired by new materials and technology. 'We must invent and rebuild our futurist city like an immense and tumultuous shipyard, active, mobile, and everywhere dynamic, and the futurist house like a gigantic machine.' The movement attracted poets, musicians, artists and architects, until several were killed after enlisting in the First World War. Although few futurist buildings were constructed, the ideas behind them were genuinely ahead of their time.

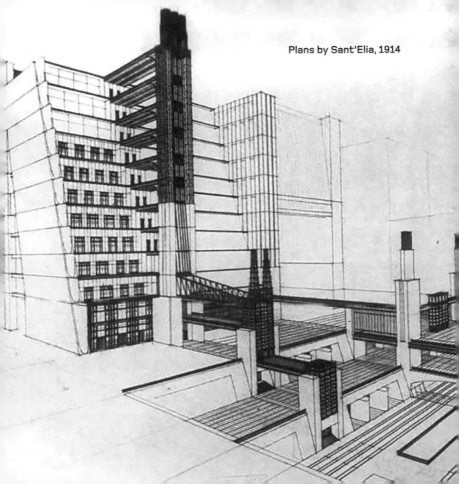

Plans by Sant'Elia, 1914

Dutch and German expressionism

With parallels in German contemporary art, expressionist architecture emerged through the ideas of Bruno Taut (1880–1938) and Hans Poelzig (1869–1936) as a counter to the formalism, rational planning and pure geometries of the Deutscher Werkbund and modernism. The movement spread across Europe after being taken up by the Dutch, Austrian, Czech and Danish avant-garde from 1910 to 1930.

Characterized by distortion, emotional ideas, sculptural forms and organic or biomorphic shapes, expressionism also took inspiration from new technical possibilities offered by mass-produced brick, steel and glass. Taut's Glass Pavilion (1914), a pointed dome of coloured panes, was a temporary construction for a Werkbund exhibition in Cologne. Economic constraints limited the number of commissions built between 1914 and 1925, and many expressionist works remained as drawings. The term now encompasses architecture of any date or location that exhibits qualities of the original movement.

Hufeisensiedlung (Horseshoe Estate) in Berlin, Taut, 1925–33

Erich Mendelsohn

The icon for expressionist architecture is the curvaceous and organic Einstein Tower in Potsdam (opposite), built by German Erich Mendelsohn (1887–1953) in 1921. Aiming for a synthesis of functionalism with expressionism, Mendelsohn blends rationality with dynamism. Specially designed to test the theories of Albert Einstein, the building was constructed from brick, concrete and block render, and includes an underground laboratory with a vertical telescope and domed observatory roof. Outcroppings at each side provide stability for the squat tower, while round windows are recessed in niches.

Although he drew on elements of modernism, Mendelsohn's architecture was individual, with curves, rhythmical forms and an imaginative use of glass, often emphasizing horizontals. Fleeing Nazi Germany in 1933, he went to Brussels and then London. With Serge Chermayeff (1900–96), he designed the De La Warr Pavilion in East Sussex (1933–5), one of Britain's first modernist buildings and a spectacular example of his style.

Gerrit Rietveld

G errit Rietveld (1888–1964) is remembered as much for his furniture as for his buildings; his simple chairs, now classics, were designed for mass production and affordability – ideas he would later carry into housing. Rietveld qualified as an architect in 1919 and joined De Stijl, a movement founded in 1917 by artists Piet Mondrian and Theo van Doesburg. De Stijl artists advocated pure abstraction: simplifying compositions to verticals and horizontals, and primary colours with black and white. In 1923, Gropius invited Rietveld to exhibit at the Bauhaus, the groundbreaking German school of arts and crafts, and in 1924 he designed the Schröder House in Utrecht (opposite), a 3D realization of a Mondrian painting. A blend of De Stijl and Bauhaus ideals, it comprises intersecting planes on the exterior and sliding walls inside to rearrange living spaces. In 1928, Rietveld broke with De Stijl in favour of a more functionalist architectural style, and in later decades pursued social housing projects, using inexpensive materials and innovative methods of prefabrication.

Walter Gropius

G ropius (1883–1969), a pivotal figure in modernism, exerted an influence matched by few of his peers in Germany – where he founded the Bauhaus – or in the United States, where he moved after the Nazis seized power. After travelling Europe to study its architecture, he worked from 1907 to 1910 for Behrens. Then in 1911–13, with Adolf Meyer, he designed the Fagus shoe last factory in Alfeld, Germany (opposite), inspired by Behrens's AEG factory. Its glazed corners, hung daringly on a steel frame, convey a sense of lightness that contrasts with the solid brick entrance. His 1913 article 'The Development of Industrial Buildings' was influential, particularly on Mendelsohn and Le Corbusier. From 1919, Gropius served as master of the Weimar arts and crafts schools and turned them into the Bauhaus, employing some of the greatest artists and designers as teachers. His Bauhaus school complex at Dessau (1925) became a landmark in functionalism. Based in Massachusetts from the 1930s, he designed a series of striking homes that helped introduce modernism to America.

Bauhaus

The most influential modernist art school of the 20th century, the Bauhaus ('house of building') took a unique approach to teaching and exerted a global impact. Its leader, Gropius, blurring distinctions between fine and applied arts, and aiming to reunite creativity and manufacturing, began by the mid-1920s to switch the focus from crafts to industrial design. Leading artists and designers taught students a wide range of arts, crafts and methods of mass-production. The curriculum included printmaking, woodwork, metalwork, ceramics and architecture, and the focus on experimentation and problem-solving had a lasting influence on arts education. In 1925 the Bauhaus moved into Gropius's purpose-built complex at Dessau, dominated by the three-storey workshop building with its full-width curtain glass wall. In 1928, the architect Hannes Meyer (1889–1954) took over from Gropius, but after incorporating his Marxist ideals, he was dismissed. In 1932, the school was moved to Berlin, under Mies van der Rohe, but it closed indefinitely when the Nazis took power in 1933.

Constructivism

Flourishing in the USSR in the 1920s and 1930s, constructivism was the means by which artists and architects intended to create a new Soviet Union, by exploiting modern materials such as steel, concrete and expanses of glass. Principles of constructivism emerged from suprematism, De Stijl and the Bauhaus. Their main aim was to bring the avant-garde into everyday life, but a shortage of funds after the Russian Revolution meant the movement remained more of an ideology than a practical movement, and few designs were built. Vladimir Tatlin (1885–1953), for instance, designed the *Monument to the Third International*, or 'Tatlin's Tower', in Petrograd (St Petersburg) in 1919–20. Though never built, this glass and steel structure was to have been a fantastic, 400-metre (1,312-ft) double spiral with a revolving cone and cylinders, to serve as headquarters of the Comintern. Konstantin Melnikov (1890–1974) designed and built the Soviet Pavilion for the 1925 Decorative Arts Exposition in Paris: a dynamic, cantilevered structure with rooms designed by Alexander Rodchenko (1891–1956).

Mosselprom
Building in Moscow,
N.D. Strukov,
1917–25

Social housing

The cramped slum housing in Europe's 19th-century cities, a legacy of the Industrial Revolution, led to generations of ill-health and high infant mortality in working families. In 1919 the British government, facing a severe housing shortage, passed an act to subsidize council building programmes. By 1921, some 170,000 low-density houses – with three bedrooms, indoor toilets and a garden – had been built for the better-off working classes. Across Europe, architects including Gropius, Taut and Martin Wagner (1885–1957) designed practical, low-cost housing solutions, with low-rise flats reaching Britain by the late 1920s. But the heavy bombing of the next war led to an even greater housing crisis. Britain's response was to throw up some 156,000 'prefabs' – short-lived, factory-built bungalows – followed by hardier homes of reinforced concrete. In the 1950s, with homes still scarce, architects now envisioned a new style of mass social housing: tower blocks, or 'streets in the sky', with communal facilities such as crèches and laundries. By the 1960s, more than 500,000 tower-block homes were built in London alone.

Karl Marx–Hof in Vienna,
Karl Ehn, 1927–30

Rationalism

The rationalist movement, popular in early 20th-century Italy, arose out of a belief that successful architecture can be interpreted by reason. In 1926, a group of young architects including Guido Frette (1901–84) Adalberto Libera (1903–63) and Giuseppe Terragni (1904–43) founded Gruppo 7 and published a manifesto in the magazine *Rassegna Italiana*, declaring: 'We do not intend to break with tradition . . . The new architecture, the true architecture, should be the result of a close association between logic and rationality.' Spurning useless ornamentation, they embraced the machine age (albeit less violently than their futurist compatriots), and were inspired by the modernist essays of Le Corbusier and Gropius. They also, however, sought to create a timeless Italian architecture. The results could be jarring: the corner of Terragni's Novocomum in Como (1927–9, opposite) featured a squared-off top floor atop a curved, glazed shaft. But they could also work effectively, as in Libera's Trento Elementary School (1931–3), whose modern lines sat comfortably with the ancient city wall.

Ludwig Mies van der Rohe

The German-born Mies van der Rohe (1886–1969), who became one of America's foremost practioners of modernism, began his career as an apprentice to Behrens in 1912 before opening his own practice in Berlin. His pioneering buildings made use of new materials, such as steel frames and glass, with extreme clarity; describing his style as 'skin and bones', he discarded ornament and opened up interior spaces. In his German Pavilion at the Barcelona Exhibition of 1929, he created a geometric arrangement of green glass, chrome columns and marble, onyx and travertine planes. His two-storey Tugendhat House (1930) features a sweeping wall of glass and onyx and ebony screens. In 1927, Mies organized the exhibition *Die Wohnung,* which showcased the best modernist thinking on the problems of social housing. He directed the Bauhaus from 1930 to 1933, then emigrated in 1938 to the United States. His influential Seagram Building (1958) in New York helped to inaugurate a new era of simple, tall buildings that showed off their structural elements rather than camouflaging them with superfluous decoration.

Farnsworth House in Plano Illinois,
Van der Rohe, 1945—51

Le Corbusier

Swiss artist, architect and urban planner Le Corbusier (1887–1965) blended modernism with bold expression. An early user of rough-cast concrete, he helped instigate the international style. Born Charles-Édouard Jeanneret-Gris (the pseudonym came in 1920), he moved to Paris after the war and met the Cubist painter Amédée Ozenfant (1886–1966). They created Purism, a new art movement, publishing a manifesto and a journal, *L'Esprit Nouveau*. In 1922, Le Corbusier opened a practice with his cousin Pierre Jeanneret (1896–1967), and they co-designed buildings and furniture for 40 years. The manifesto stated his 'five points of architecture' – supporting pilotis (piers), roof gardens, open-plan interiors, ornament-free façades, and full-length horizontal windows – and his designs bore them out. Following his own principle that 'a house is a machine for living in', he created fluent, light-filled interiors in such designs as Citrohan House in Stuttgart (1922) and Villa Savoye, Paris (opposite, 1928–31). His Marseille housing complex, Unité d'Habitation (1952), is a landmark in brutalist architecture.

Art deco

Derived from such diverse influences as African, Aztec, ancient Egyptian, futurism and cubism, art deco manifested in most fields of design. Taking its name from the International Exposition of Modern Decorative and Industrial Arts, held in Paris in 1925, where the style was first exhibited, art deco was modern and opulent, and its geometric motifs contrasted sharply with the fluid signatures of art nouveau. Buildings are often embellished with hard-edged, low-relief designs in stepped patterns, chevrons and sunburst patterns; prominent materials include chrome, glass, lacquer and inlaid wood. The style endured throughout the Depression because it was practical, clean-cut and optimistic. Epitomizing the machine age, it appeared in streamline moderne designs (see page 326) including New York's Chrysler Building (opposite, 1928–30 designed by William Van Alen (1883–1954) and the Empire State Building (1930) designed by William F. Lamb (1893–1952). In New Zealand, the coastal town of Napier, devasted by the 1931 earthquake, was largely rebuilt in the art deco style.

De Stijl

Originating in the Netherlands with Piet Mondrian (1872–1944) and Theo Van Doesburg (1883–1931), De Stijl ('the style') sought to create the ideal fusion of form and function, a reduction of elements to create harmony and order, in the wake of the First World War. Adopting the visual elements of cubism and constructivism, as well as the mystical geometric principles of mathematician M.H.J. Schoenmaekers (1875–1944), it aimed for a new aesthetic that would encompass all the arts, including painting, architecture, urban planning, industrial design, typography, music and poetry.In architecture, De Stijl helped to instigate the international style of the 1920s and 1930s and had a marked influence on the more revolutionary architects, including Mies van der Rohe and Le Corbusier. Architect members of the group included Rietveld, whose Schröder House (opposite, 1924) in Utrecht was the only building completed to pure De Stijl principles, and J.J.P. Oud (1890–1963), whose 1925 Café De Unie in Rotterdam features rectangular planes in primary colours and white plaster, like a giant Mondrian painting.

Streamline moderne

Streamline moderne (also called art moderne) originated in the functional aesthetic of the Bauhaus, and rose to popularity in the 1930s, particularly in the US. It was in part a less decorative outgrowth of art deco, but was also a product of its time, fusing the pared-down austerity of the Depression with the efficiency, dynamism and speed embodied in the new machine age. Technological advances, smooth and powerful machines, high-speed transportation and innovative construction methods all filtered into the style, which went on show at the 1933 World Fair in Chicago and permeated all areas of design, from trains to toasters. Streamline moderne buildings have an aerodynamic look: rounded corners, often wrapped with strong horizontals and long bands of windows; ocean liner-type balconies; porthole windows. Eschewing the bright colours sometimes seen in art deco, most streamline moderne buildings have smooth white-plastered exteriors. Robert V. Derrah's (1894–1946) Coca-Cola Building in Los Angeles (1939) resembles an ocean liner, set off with minimal red branding.

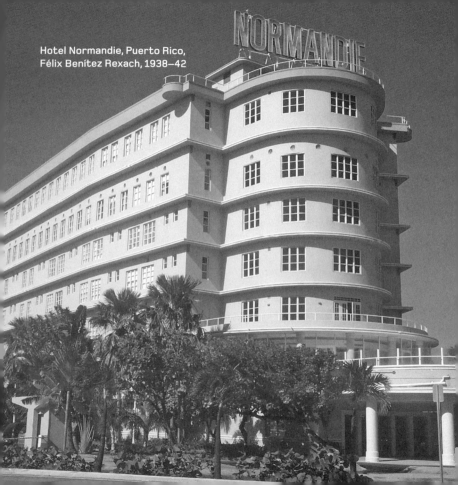

Hotel Normandie, Puerto Rico,
Félix Benítez Rexach, 1938–42

Concrete

By the early 20th century, concrete buildings were becoming as prevalent as steel structures. From its use in sinuous art nouveau forms, such as Gaudí's Sagrada Familia, to more angular structures, such as the Bahá'í House of Worship (opposite, 1912) in Illinois, designed by Louis Bourgeois (1856–1930), concrete could create curving, arched and sculptural designs, a notable example being Mendelsohn's expressionist Einstein Tower.

Le Corbusier was the first architect to make wide use of poured and reinforced concrete, after working in Paris with Auguste Perret (1874–1954), a pioneer in reinforced concrete construction, and later with Behrens. From his early unbuilt designs for Maison Dom-ino (1914–15), to the chapel of Notre Dame du Haut at Ronchamp, France (1954), Le Corbusier was fascinated by concrete's adaptability, and by its sculptural and structural potential for relatively little cost. Reinforced concrete became a favourite of many modern architects, including Oscar Niemeyer, Paul Rudolph (1918–97), Tadao Ando and Santiago Calatrava.

International style

Among the radical 20th-century ideas that spread from Europe to the United States was the international style, named at a 1932 exhibition at New York's Museum of Modern Art. It was called *Modern Architecture: International Exhibition*, and the architecture on display reflected the strong influence of the Bauhaus. The curators – architect/critic Philip Johnson and historian/critic Henry-Russell Hitchcock – wrote the accompanying catalogue, *The International Style: Architecture since 1922*, including work by Gropius, Rietveld, Le Corbusier and Mies van der Rohe. Hitchcock and Johnson identified three main principles of the international style: the expression of volume rather than mass, the emphasis on balance rather than symmetry and the abandonment of applied ornament. It was simple, honest and functional, utilizing steel, glass, reinforced concrete and chrome, with open interior spaces, white stucco walls, rectilinear forms, flat roofs and horizontal ribbon windows. In other words, it distilled the essence of European modernism or functionalism.

Villa Savoy interior,
Le Corbusier 1928–31

Philip Johnson

Remembered in his obituary as 'the elder statesman and enfant terrible of American architecture', Philip Johnson (1906–2005) spent his early years championing modernism and its exponents, particularly Mies van der Rohe and Gropius; he would later work with Mies, notably on the Seagram Building (1958). Another key influence on Johnson was Le Corbusier. In 1930, Johnson founded the Department of Architecture and Design at New York's Museum of Modern Art, where the 1932 exhibition he put on with Hitchcock introduced America to the international style. After graduating in architecture, he designed for his own use the Glass House (1949) in New Canaan; an archetype in the international style, its spare rectangle of glass and steel encloses an airily open interior. Johnson later explored other styles, and his partnership with John Burgee (b.1933) from 1967 to 1991 sired a string of postmodernist landmarks including the trapezoid towers of Pennzoil Place (1976) in Houston, the broken-pedimented AT&T building (1984) in New York, and the aptly nicknamed Lipstick Building (1986), also New York.

One PPG Place
in Pittsburgh,
Johnson, 1981–4

Seagram Building

In 1958, Mies van der Rohe built a 38-storey steel and glass tower in Manhattan for the Seagram distillery head office, setting new standards for modern skyscrapers. Abandoning all exterior decoration, the building is in the international style; a glossy monolith rising 157 metres (515 ft) above the granite plaza below. Often quoted as saying 'God is in the details', Mies zealously concentrated on the smallest elements of the structure, which combines a steel frame, a core of steel and reinforced concrete, and a glass skin. The frame had to be covered with fireproofing to satisfy the building code, so Mies – keen to have a structure on show – added 1,500 tonnes of non-structural bronze I-beams, which are visible through the amber-tinted glass. Mies had evolved a completely rational approach, designing 'universal' spaces enclosed in rectangular blocks, and evoking classical elements – the division into base, shaft and capital; the use of bronze – to create a sense of timeless serenity. The double-height travertine lobby and grand restaurant are designed by Philip Johnson.

Richard Neutra

Austrian-born Richard Neutra (1892–1970) began his career in Switzerland and Germany before moving to the United States in 1923. There, he worked for Frank Lloyd Wright, and then with Rudolf Schindler (1887–1953) in California. Early international style buildings in the Los Angeles area include the Lovell House (opposite, 1929), consisting of a series of overlapping planes, and (with his son, Dion) the Neutra Research House (1932), a glass house with roof garden.

Through a series of private commissions, Neutra earned rapid acclaim for his unusual attention to the needs of his clients, and a flexible approach to the tenets of modernism. Many of his buildings also gained fame through the images of photographer Julius Schulman (1910–2009), whose portfolio immortalized the Californian mid-century lifestyle. In 1949, Neutra formed a partnership with Robert E. Alexander (1935–93), which enabled him to design larger commercial and institutional buildings such as the now-demolished Cyclorama at Gettysburg, Pennsylvania.

Alvar Aalto

Finnish architect, artist and designer Alvar Aalto (1898–1976) created buildings, furniture, textiles and glassware. His early career paralleled the rapid economic growth and industrialization of Finland during the first half of the 20th century, and his style developed from a form of classicism, through modernism in the 1930s, to a more organic, Nordic-inspired style from the 1940s. The Alvar Aalto Museum that he designed in his home city of Jyväskylä (1973) exemplifies his 'white period', as his later style is often known. His first public buildings – the Jyväskylä Workers' Club (1925), the Jyväskylä Defence Corps building (1926) and the Seinäjoki Defence Corps building (1924–9) – fuse neoclassicism with elements of modernism. His Viipuri Library (1927–35) in Vyborg, Russia, comprises two offset white rectangles, with an interior of natural materials, warm colours and undulating lines. His Säynätsalo Town Hall (opposite, 1951) is an innovative, organic, brick-built series of buildings, with 'butterfly trusses' supporting the main hall roof, arranged around a glazed central courtyard.

Louis Kahn

N oted for his expressive use of concrete and brick, Louis I. Kahn (1901–74) was one of the leading American architects of the 20th century. First opening his practice in 1935, he took a professorship at Yale in 1947. In 1950–1, inspired by a term as architect in residence at the American Academy in Rome, he began to mix the solid forms and stable materials of antiquity with modern innovations; the results can be seen in, for instance, the barrel-vaulted ceilings of the Kimbell Art Museum, Texas (opposite, 1966–72). The campus of the Salk Institute for Biological Studies in San Diego (1962–3) is arguably his masterpiece: a complex of buildings in pinkish concrete (mixed to an old Roman recipe), separated by a stream of water coursing through a serene plaza, it was designated an historic landmark in 1991. Major projects on the Indian subcontinent included the National Assembly Building of Bangladesh in Dhaka (1962–83), a remarkable geometric design that maximizes natural light in all parts of the building including the vast parliament chamber.

Segregated planning

By the 1920s, car ownership was soaring, radically altering the dynamic of towns and cities. The garden cities of the late 19th and early 20th centuries had integrated green open spaces, but insufficient provision for private vehicles; as cars proliferated, new city planners began zoning to meet motorists' needs. In 1929, the model town of Radburn in New Jersey followed England's garden cities, but was established specifically 'as a town for the motor age'. As shown opposite, it had paths, underpasses and bridges that segregated pedestrians from the traffic flow. This isolation continued with residential areas laid out in 'super blocks', incorporating networks of cul-de-sacs that provided peace and privacy. Because Radburn was built during the Depression, the ideas took a while to spread; but some were adopted early on by the CIAM (International Congresses of Modern Architecture), a group that applied social and urban planning issues to modern architecture. Segregated planning took off more widely around the world during the 1950s and 1960s.

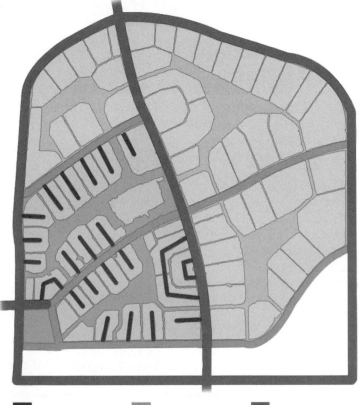

 Local street   Through street   ■ Boulevard

Oscar Niemeyer

Oscar Niemeyer (1907–2012) became a pioneer of modernist architecture, introducing it to his home country of Brazil from the 1940s onwards, and was the first modernist from a country beyond Europe or North America to achieve global fame. Niemeyer often used large expanses of glass and curvilinear forms, but in contrast with the Germanic 'glass box' of modernism, his buildings were expressive and sinuous. His designs for the new capital city, Brasília, were noted for their free-flowing lines (opposite). Niemeyer's early works show Le Corbusier's influence, but he gradually formulated his own style, and specialized in light, rounded forms that create a sense of harmony and elegance. He explored the aesthetic possibilities of reinforced concrete in skyscrapers, exhibition centres, residential areas, theatres, offices, universities and hospitals; the Itamaraty Palace (1962–70) in Brasília, for instance, features rough concrete arches that appear to float on the surrounding pool, and a seemingly unsupported cascade of spiralling stairs in the atrium.

Sydney Opera House

In 1956, the government of New South Wales announced an international competition to design a new opera house for Sydney. The site was to be a promontory with views to the sea and the Harbour Bridge. The winning design, from a little-known Danish architect, Jørn Utzon (1918–2008), featured overlapping white roofs that covered the building's two main halls, seeming to emerge from the water and resembling the sails of giant yachts; Utzon claimed he was inspired by the act of peeling an orange. But when the design led to structural problems, Utzon replaced his elliptical shells with a new concept based on sections of a sphere. The Opera House, though controversial among the public, became an icon of Sydney and is today one of the world's most recognizable buildings. Its glass walls are secured by vertical steel mullions, and chevron-patterned ceramic tiles cover the sculptural roofs. Inside, high vaulted ceilings are covered in curving plywood panels, and canopies of glass held by steel ribs cover the foyers and bars – inspired, according to Utzon, by birds' wings.

Eero Saarinen

The son of an influential Finnish architect, Eero Saarinen (1910–61) worked for most of his life in the United States. After spending the Second World War designing for the military, he took over the family firm in Michigan, creating buildings that blended his father's Art Deco style with his own modernist ideas. The result was a simple but rich sculptural approach offering more visual drama than the austerity of the international style.

Among several prestigious buildings, Saarinen designed the TWA Flight Centre (1956–62) at John F. Kennedy Airport in New York, the Kresge Auditorium at MIT in Massachusetts (opposite, 1953–5) and the Jefferson National Expansion Memorial in Missouri (1947–66, including the iconic Gateway Arch). Many feature his characteristic thin-shelled concrete curves, steel, large amounts of glass and minimal interior supports. Alongside his architectural work, Saarinen became equally renowned as a designer of modernist furniture.

I.M. Pei

Ieoh Ming Pei (b.1917) moved to the United States from China in his teens, studying design at Harvard under Gropius and eventually establishing his own firm in 1955. His modernist designs used expressive geometric forms that incorporated large expanses of glass, and often recall cubist art.

Pei's landmark buildings include the J. F. Kennedy Library in Boston (1965–79), a nine-storey glass and concrete structure; the East Building of the National Gallery of Art in Washington DC (1968–78), comprising overlapping triangular forms that complement the existing neoclassical building; and the monumental reflective-glass Bank of China Tower in Hong Kong (1982–8). He also executed the West Wing and renovation of the Museum of Fine Arts in Boston (1981 and 1986). Perhaps his most famous and controversial commission, however, was a new entrance to the Louvre in Paris (opposite, 1983–89), a bold glass and steel pyramid above a subterranean lobby that provides a spectacular stylistic contrast with the palatial museum itself.

Metabolism

Metabolism was the most influential architectural movement to emerge from postwar Japan. In a nation undergoing rapid economic revival, yet still subject to natural disasters, Metabolism's practitioners envisioned it as a way to design cities and buildings in organic and repeatable ways, essentially in imitation of nature.

Those involved included Kiyonori Kikutake (1928–2011), Kisho Kurokawa (1934–2007) and Fumihiko Maki (b.1928); it was at the suggestion of their mentor, noted architect Kenzo Tange (1913–2005), that they founded Metabolism at the 1960 Tokyo World Design Conference. They created visionary designs of floating cities, spiralling structures, and flexible buildings that could be expanded in modular ways. Many were too ambitious ever to be built; but their approach is illustrated in Kurokawa's Nakagin Capsule Tower (opposite, 1970–2) in Tokyo; designed for both residential and office use, it comprises 140 identical concrete and steel capsules bolted to two armature towers.

Structural expressionism

Structural expressionism was a reaction to the minimalist aesthetic embodied by the plain, sleek forms of modernism. Emerging in the 1970s in Europe and North America, its aim was to allow structural elements to dictate the aesthetic of a building, and by extension to use original approaches to obtaining structural stability. Structural expressionist buildings incorporated the latest technological innovations and interchangeable, prefabricated parts for flexibility in design and economy in construction. Some feature their structural elements on the outside as well as the inside – for example, with exposed steel frames cladding concrete walls. Main practitioners of the style include Colombian-American Bruce Graham (1925–2010) and Bangladeshi Fazlur Rahman Khan (1929–82). Under the watch of Skidmore, Owings & Merrell, both men worked on a pair of iconic Chicago skyscrapers: the John Hancock Building (1968, opposite), clad in a 'trussed tube' of x-braces, and the Onterie Center (1986), braced diagonally with concrete panels.

Postmodernism

Brazen, varied, vibrant, and playful, postmodernism emerged in the late 1960s as a direct reaction to the restraint and discernment of modernism and functionalism. The movement evolved simultaneously in the arts, philosophy and architecture: in the latter its presence was felt through the increased use of decoration, idiosyncratic and humorous design and blocks of colour in preference to the relatively austere modernist materials of steel, glass and reinforced concrete.

The movement began in North America, instigated by Robert Venturi, who asserted that architecture should be more complex and cryptic. Others associated with postmodernism include Philip Johnson, Michael Graves, James Stirling and Frank Gehry. As well as abandoning modernist austerity, postmodern architects have often used modern materials and techniques to subvert expectations – for example adding incongruous and non-functional traditional features to modern buildings or creating what seem to be unstable structures.

National-Nederlanden Building in Prague,
Gehry, 1992—6

Robert Venturi

After working briefly with Saarinen and Kahn, Robert Venturi (b.1925) entered academia and soon became known as an outspoken critic of bland modernism, and the chief advocate of a more complex and playful, postmodern approach to architecture. Establishing his own practice in 1960, many of his subsequent projects also involved his wife and partner the architect and planner Denise Scott Brown (b.1931). His book *Complexity and Contradiction in Architecture* (written 1962, published 1966) became one of the most influential architectural texts since Le Corbusier's 1923 *Towards a New Architecture*.

In 1961–4, Venturi designed the Vanna Venturi House for his mother in Pennsylvania; though modest in scale, its incongruous blending of a giant broken-pediment façade, big chimney, pitched pop-top roof and ironic entrance arch set the postmodern agenda. The couple also designed the Sainsbury Wing (1985–91) of London's National Gallery, echoing original elements of the neoclassical building in a fresh way (opposite).

Brutalism

Brutalism's name, from the French term *béton brut* ('rough concrete') puns on the style's 'brutal' aspects that polarized opinion in its 1950 to 1970s heyday. Proponents saw it as a riposte to the blandness of modernism, but critics decry its cold, totalitarian look. Brutalist architecture is strong-looking and dominated by raw, exposed concrete, or steel and brick or rough-hewn stone, often with repeated modular elements. Its low cost saw it taken up around the world for institutional buildings and housing estates during the post-war era. The influential 1956 London exhibition *This is Tomorrow*, featuring artists, musicians and architects, included several exponents of brutalism: James Stirling, Ernó Goldfinger (1902–87) and Alison (1928–94) and Peter (1923–2003) Smithson. Le Corbusier famously used *béton brut* for his Unité d'Habitation in France (1952) and 1953 Secretariat Building in Chandigarh, India. Notable brutalist buildings in the United States include the Yale Art & Architecture Building (1963) by Paul Rudolph and Le Corbusier's Carpenter Center at Harvard (also 1963).

Trellick Tower in London,
Goldfinger, 1966–72

Habitat

As part of Montreal's Expo 1967 world fair, Canadian-Israeli architect Moshe Safdie (b.1938) created a built environment of 158 apartments as his first major work. He had worked on the idea when preparing his university thesis. Inspired by clustered ancient hill homes in Italy, Spain and the Middle East, the apartments are constructed from 354 individual prefabricated concrete units, each stacked in seemingly haphazard arrangements, and connected by internal steel cables. The scheme fulfilled Safdie's vision of affordable, mass-produced family housing. Known as Habitat, the structure has the appearance of an arbitrary stack of boxes, but in reality Safdie planned the arrangement to feature rhythmic projections and recessions, and to create areas of privacy and light. An environmentally sensitive air-conditioning system also provides water for a series of terraced swimming pools. After the world fair, Habitat became one of the most fashionable addresses in Montreal, an example of both brutalism and architectural pop art.

Neorationalism

Also called *la tendenza*, neorationalism developed in the 1960s and 1970s, led by Italian architect and theoretician Aldo Rossi (1931–97), who advocated a reinvigoration of classicism in place of modernism, functionalism and postmodernism. Inspired by the paintings of Giorgio de Chirico (1888–1978), especially the dramatic perspectives, arcades and arches, squares and long streets, Rossi addressed many of these issues in his book *The Architecture of the City* (1966). From Italy, the movement progressed to Spain, France and Germany, focusing on the past and ignoring enthusiasms for new styles. It was the first truly Italian architectural movement since 1945 (when a large reconstruction programme was undertaken). Neorationalists included Álvaro Siza (b.1933), Mario Botta (b.1943), Henri Ciriani (b.1936) and Oswald Mathias Ungers (1926–2007). Drawing on historical knowledge, they designed imaginative buildings, aiming to reconnect the people through a built environment that would be more in step with contemporary needs.

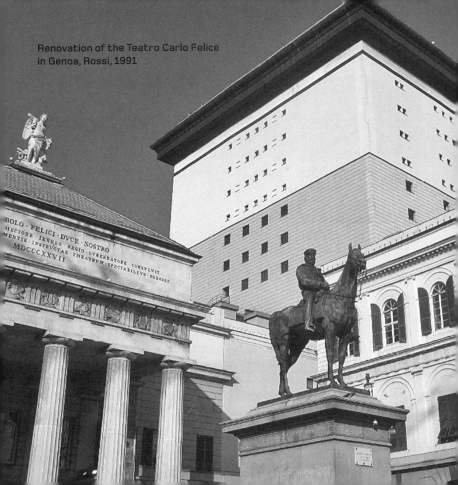

Renovation of the Teatro Carlo Felice
in Genoa, Rossi, 1991

Inside out

Redressing Mies van der Rohe's maxim 'less is more,' Venturi declared 'less is a bore'. It was intended to be flippant, but it endured in the light of postmodernism. Though it merely expressed his observation that styles come and go, Venturi's phrase came to be seen as encompassing many buildings that ignored architectural norms, such as the Pompidou Centre in Paris (1971–77), designed by Renzo Piano, Richard Rogers and Gianfranco Franchini (1938–2009). The huge modern art museum is a particularly overt example of what became known as an 'inside out' design – or 'bowellism'. Created as a monument to the late French president Georges Pompidou (1911–74), the multi-storey Pompidou Centre (opposite) is supported by an exoskeleton, and all elements that would normally be concealed inside, such as heating and cooling ducts, water pipes and electrical wiring, are on the outside, making space for the open-plan interiors. Each element is independent of all the others; even the escalators that zigzag up the façade can be shortened or lengthened as needed.

Michael Graves

One of the most important exponents of postmodernism, Michael Graves (1934–2015) began by creating modernist white geometric volumes; in the late 1960s he was classed as one of the New York Five, a group of influential East Coast modernists. Yet by the late 1970s, he sought a more diverse expression. In 1977, he designed Plocek House in New Jersey: a building reminiscent of an Italian palazzo, with classical yet abstracted columns and an exaggerated entrance arch. The use of colour, and small windows in place of large expanses of glass, signposted his move to postmodernism. In 1979–82, he designed the Portland Building in Oregon, with colourful façades decorated with a stylized garland and pilasters (opposite). The building's flamboyance and dark interiors created by small windows initially caused great controversy. His 26-storey Humana Building (1982–5) in Louisville has a granite and marble façade, and his El Gouna Resort Hotel (1995) in Egypt features rendered concrete, domed roofs and chimney-like projections, blending postmodern elements with vernacular architecture.

Norman Foster

Acclaimed for his modernist designs and technological innovations, Sir Norman Foster (b.1935) leads one of the world's most famous architectural firms. Foster + Partners' vast number of projects around the world are characterized by their use of glass, stainless steel, exposed areas and unexpected forms. Key works include the iconic Hong Kong and Shanghai Bank Headquarters in Hong Kong (1979–86, opposite), built from five structural modules that were prefabricated in Scotland, and Berlin's Reichstag building (1992–9, resurrected from the old neoclassical German parliament). Other famous projects include the vast terminal building of Hong Kong International Airport (1991–98) and 30 St Mary Axe in London (2000–03, better known by its nickname of The Gherkin). Foster's buildings are often distinguished by the use of revolutionary and ecologically conscious elements. For example the HSBC building's vast ten-storey atrium is lit by a mirrored central sun-scoop, while the Reichstag's glass dome has an automated sunshade, as well as a spiral ramp that provides panoramic views of the city.

Minimalism

The idea that freedom from clutter should be the aim of all design goes back to the late 19th century, but it was not until the mid-20th century that the need to reduce elements and ornamentation really took hold. Minimalism was an important element of the modernist project from the outset, but notions of simplicity and purity in design developed further in the United States in the 1960s as some – artists as well as architects – reacted against what they saw as chaos in abstract expressionist art. Emerging more strongly in the 1980s, minimalist architecture never developing into a defined movement: merely a number of notable buildings around the world, such as Majorca's ochre-coloured Neuendorf House (1987–9) by John Pawson (b.1949) and Claudio Silvestrin (b.1954). The Burgo Tower in Porto (opposite, 2007) by Edouardo Souto de Moura (b.1952) juxtaposes vertical and horizontal elements, while the New Art Museum (2007) in New York, by Kazuyo Sejima (b.1956), is a stack of white boxes in various sizes and heights, giving the impression of a dynamic composition of giant cubes.

Tadao Ando

From his earliest designs, the self-taught minimalist Japanese architect Tadao Ando (b.1941) demonstrated his grasp of the traditional *sukiya* style, with its use of natural materials, balanced proportions and serene ambiance – such as in his tiny Azuma House (1976) in Osaka, connected by an open air bridge, or the Matsumoto House in Ashiya (1976–7), also known as the Wall House, with its concrete frame spanned by half-tunnel vaulting. Ando has continued to design public and commercial complexes with the same traditional spirit and his own perceptions of minimalism and nature. Often using concrete or natural wood, his style is said to create a 'haiku' effect, emphasizing empty space and simplicity, while also melding with the environment. His Church on the Water (1988) in Tomamu, the Literature Museum (1989, opposite) in Himeji and the Water Temple (1991) on Awaji Island, for instance, all use sheets of water in imaginative ways. Convinced that architecture can change cities and reform society, Ando has been influential through his constantly evolving designs and prolific writing.

James Stirling

Inspired equally by Le Corbusier and the neoclassicists Schinkel, Friedrich Weinbrenner (1766–1826) and Gottfried Semper (1803–79), Glasgow-born James Stirling (1926–92) was arguably one of the most influential architects of his era. In the 1970s, he revitalized modernism using local materials and playful ideas, producing large-scale urban projects, including the Neue Staatsgalerie in Stuttgart in 1977–84. The undulating, dynamic building (opposite) is inspired by Schinkel's Altes Museum in Berlin (1828) and Wright's Guggenheim Museum in New York. His Clore Gallery (1980–7) for the Tate Britain in London is light, airy and minimalist, while his Tate Liverpool (1984) was formerly a seven-storey warehouse; leaving the exterior of the building almost untouched, Stirling transformed the interior into an arrangement of simple, elegant galleries. Stirling's final building, built on a wedge of land in the heart of the City of London, was the postmodernist No. 1 Poultry (1988–98); almost aggressively brash, it has a distinctive striped limestone façade, cylindrical clock tower and colourful courtyard.

Deconstructivism

The exponents of deconstructivism, which emerged around 1990, created spectacular forms that expressed their opposition to the ordered rationality of modernism and postmodernism. The name derived from the exhibition *Deconstructivist Architecture*, organized in New York by Philip Johnson in 1988, which featured the work of Frank Gehry (1929–), Peter Eisenman (b.1932), Rem Koolhaas (b.1944), Bernard Tschumi (b.1944), Daniel Libeskind (b.1946), Zaha Hadid (1950–) and the cooperative Coop Himmelb(l)au.

Deconstructivism is confrontational, bold and surprising. Tschumi coined the movement's motto as 'form follows fantasy' after Louis Sullivan's famous 'form follows function' (see page 282). Inspired by sources as diverse as the Russian constructivists and the theories of French philosopher Jacques Derrida, deconstructivist buildings are characterized by fragmentation, an interest in manipulating surfaces, and non-rectilinear shapes that seem to distort and dislocate the design.

Groninger Museum Pavilion, Coop Himmelb(l)au, 1994

Frank Gehry

Some of the most important works of contemporary architecture have been produced by Canadian-born Frank Gehry (b.1929), who combines both innovative and ordinary materials with expressive, often startling forms. Moving to Los Angeles in 1949, he won acclaim for his exuberant, unique structures, from cubist-inspired early buildings to the more curvilinear later works. One of his most celebrated achievements is the titanium-clad Guggenheim Museum in Bilbao (opposite, 1991–7), which appears as an intrinsic part of the urban surroundings, and also as a sculpture. A similarly sculptural design is his Vitra Design Museum (1987–9) in Weil am Rhein, Germany, clad in white stucco and zinc, which jumbles horizontals and verticals. His acoustically sophisticated, curving stainless-steel Walt Disney Concert Hall in Los Angeles (1999–2003) has become a landmark, and his Nationale-Nederlanden building in Prague (1992–6), known as the 'Dancing House' or 'Fred and Ginger', was a collaboration with Vlado Milunić (b.1941) and appears to dance between its baroque and art nouveau neighbours.

Richard Rogers

British structural expressionist Richard Rogers (b.1933) began his career exploring ideas about prefabrication; his concept of the 'zip up' house used standardized components to create energy-efficient buildings. However, he is acclaimed today for his innovative designs, including the Pompidou Centre in Paris (designed with Renzo Piano) and the Lloyd's Building (1978–86, opposite) in London, both examples of 'inside out'. The European Court of Human Rights in Strasbourg features two huge steel drums accessed through a glass-walled atrium.

His Millennium Dome (1999) in London, made of coated glass fibre and supported by 100-metre (328-ft) yellow towers, formed the core of a plan to regenerate part of the city, while his Senedd, the National Assembly for Wales in Cardiff (built 2001–6), has a glass façade, steel roof and wooden ceiling, and was designed to be sustainable. It was not to be an 'insular, closed edifice', he said, but 'a transparent envelope, looking outwards to Cardiff Bay and beyond'.

Skidmore, Owings & Merrill

One of the largest architectural firms in the world, Skidmore, Owings & Merrill was formed in Chicago in the 1930s by Louis Skidmore (1897–1962), Nathaniel Owings (1903–84) and John O. Merrill (1896–1975). It has since employed numerous outstanding architects, produced thousands of buildings and products and exerted an important influence on urban planning.

Famous for its inventiveness, the firm has produced a roll-call of world-renowned designs, such as the John Hancock Building in Chicago, a tapered rectangular tube standing 100 storeys tall (see also page 354). The Willis or Sears Tower (opposite, 1970–3), also in Chicago, employs the 'bundled tube' system – an innovation from one of the firm's partners, Fazlur Rahman Khan, that has revolutionized tall building design. Comprising a matrix of nine 'tubes' bound together, the Willis Tower was for 25 years the world's tallest skyscraper, a title now held by the firm's 163-storey, 829.8-metre (2,722-ft) Burj Khalifa in Dubai (see page 400).

Renzo Piano

Italian architect and engineer Renzo Piano (b.1937) was cited by *TIME* magazine in 2006 as one of the world's 100 most influential people. An habitual collaborator, he worked for Louis Kahn in Philadelphia, with Richard Rogers (notably producing the Pompidou Centre) and with engineer Peter Rice (1935–92) before setting up his own independent firm in 1981.

Piano's portfolio is hugely diverse in both style, materials and techniques used, but is always concerned with habitability and sustainability. The Menil Collection Museum in Houston (1982) is a low, articulated box of concrete reinforced with steel girders. In 2006 he extended the Morgan Library in Manhattan, using a deliberately plain design so as not to detract from the original 1903 building. His California Academy of Sciences in San Francisco (2008) has a 'living roof' that is vital to the building's heating and cooling efficiency. The Shard in London (opposite) – a giant, pyramidal glass spire rising 309.6 metres (1,016ft) from a tiny split-level site – was completed in 2012.

Expressive rationalism

Dating from the 1990s, expressive rationalism is neither a consistent architectural style nor a conscious approach. It is more a product of capitalism and mass-consumerism, and developed simultaneously in various parts of the world as the needs of cities changed in the late 20th and early 21st centuries. Although it follows on from modernism in that it furnishes cities, the two differ: expressive rationalism is complex, the buildings are usually used by large numbers (and are thus large in dimensions), and the designs are often achieved through computer modelling and advanced engineering. Herzog & de Meuron's 'Bird's Nest' National Stadium for the 2008 Olympic games in Beijing is an example. With a complex, asymmetrical mesh of steel making up the walls, roof and stairs, it has an inner skin of plastic and a transparent membrane roof. It is also full of Chinese symbolism. On its artificial island in Dubai, Burj al Arab (opposite, 1994–9) is a hotel designed by British architect Tom Wright (b.1957) to resemble a giant yacht's sail and to symbolize luxury, wealth and power.

Zaha Hadid

Visionary Iraqi-British architect Zaha Hadid (b.1950) is celebrated for her use of vast, arching forms and creative use of materials in buildings, product design and furniture. Using unexpected spatial concepts, her buildings incorporate unusual, asymmetrical angles and perspectives, combining tiers, diagonals and fragmented geometry. As the first female recipient of many leading awards, she has blazed a trail for women working in architecture.

Amongst her most notable designs are the Vitra Fire Station (1990–3) in Weil am Rhein, Germany, with concrete planes at dynamic angles that create a sense of tension and urgency; the dramatically curved and angled Bergisel Ski Jump (2002) in Innsbruck; and the Rosenthal Centre for Contemporary Arts in Cincinnati (2003), which has a massive glass curtain wall. The Bridge Pavilion in Zaragoza, Spain (opposite) is a 280-metre (919-ft) covered bridge that formed the centrepiece of the city's hosting of the international Expo 2008.

Herzog & de Meuron

The famed Basel architectural firm Herzog & de Meuron was founded in 1978 by Jacques Herzog (b.1950) and Pierre de Meuron (b.1950). They are known for innovative designs using new materials and techniques, as well as creative interpretations; after transforming a disused power station into London's Tate Modern art museum in 2000, they added a new adjacent building in 2016, juxtaposing refined with raw and old with new, and utilizing dramatic angles and strip windows. The Tate extension bears comparison to their 2005 addition to the Walker Art Center in Minneapolis – a folded volume clad in aluminium. In 2004, they built the Forum Building in Barcelona, Spain, with bulging masses and cantilevered corners. Their Allianz Arena football stadium in Munich (opposite, 2005) features a quilted white plastic exterior that metamorphoses under different lighting effects. The partners' imaginative responses to unique design problems reflect their sympathies with fine art, and in the past they have collaborated with artists such as Gerhard Richter (b.1932) and Rémy Zaugg (1943–2005).

Creative reuse

In its new embodiment, London's Tate Modern art museum (opposite) is a successful example of creative reuse in architecture – also called adaptive reuse or architectural conservation. Formerly Bankside Power Station and built originally in 1891, the building became redundant a century later and was destined for demolition until British writer and architectural historian Gavin Stamp (b.1948) made a plea for it to be saved. Across the world, increasingly, structures that no longer serve their original purpose are being reused creatively through the application of new methods and materials. Although it is often more cost-effective to demolish a building and replace it, heritage is taken into account. Creative reuse can involve approaches ranging from reconstruction, restoration and conservation to radical new structural additions. The Pratt Street Power Plant in Baltimore, USA, was closed in 1973 but reworked for the 21st century into shops, restaurants and offices. In Duisburg, Germany, the Thyssen Steelworks was reinvented by Latz + Partner in 1999 as a public leisure space.

Biomimetics

Biomimetics – from the Greek meaning 'imitation of life' – describes the study of biological structures, processes and behaviours, and its application in various fields, such as product design or structural engineering. Observing how natural organisms adapt to their environments can help create efficient and/or sustainable designs (on the premise that if nature has honed a design over millions of years, it must be good). Natural structures have long inspired architects; for instance, the fan vaulting in church naves (from medieval times to Gaudí's Sagrada Familia, opposite) mimics the branching of tree canopies. Other examples that borrow structurally from nature include the Eden Project (2001) in Cornwall, modelled after soap bubbles and pollen grains, and Foster's Gherkin Tower (2003) in London, with a hexagonal skin inspired by a marine sponge. The Eastgate Centre in Harare (1996), by local architect Mick Pearce (b.1938), was designed to mimic the natural thermal control of a termite mound, as an alternative to using air-conditioning systems.

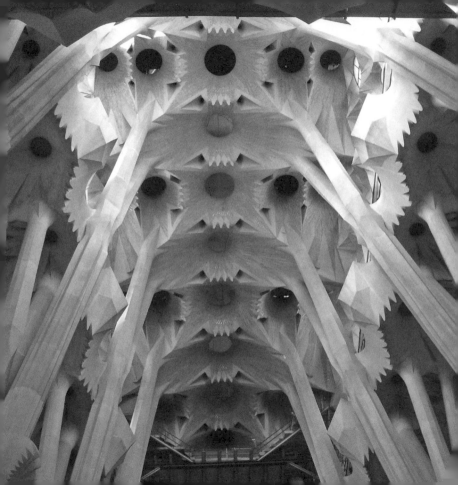

Sustainable design

In light of environmental concerns, there are increasing calls for architecture to be sustainable or green. Over the lifespan of a large building, the processes of construction, maintenance and demolition use a lot of energy and resources, alongside the energy used for heating, cooling and lighting in normal operation. But where buildings are concerned, younger doesn't always mean greener: a 2012 report on New York City's buildings found that the Empire State Building (1931) was more efficient than the supposedly 'green' 7 World Trade Center (2008). Much modern architecture is energy-inefficient on account of its expansive glazing and thin walls, and a frequent prioritization of style over resilient or sustainable design. For architecture to retain its credibility, it must conserve the Earth's finite resources, reduce energy consumption, manage waste more effectively and create buildings that work with the environment. Sydney's One Central Park (opposite, 2010–13) for example, incorporates natural lighting technology, 'hanging gardens', and other sustainable technology such as reainwater retention and recycling systems.

Burj Khalifa

Serving as offices, residential apartments and a hotel, the Burj Khalifa, named after the ruler of Abu Dhabi and president of the UAE, is the tallest building in the world at 829.8 metres (2,722 ft) high. Despite its unique appearance, designed to attract international notice, the structure is built on conventional construction methods, albeit modified to cope with the building's unique demands.

The Y-shaped plan is formed by three wings connected to a central core, which makes it ultra-stable. The wings contain the residential units and hotel guest rooms, and the central core supports the colossal height of the building as well as housing all the elevators and mechanical systems. Rising above this reinforced concrete section of the building is the structural steel spire, which is decorated with traditional Islamic forms. The spire also highlights the tower's resemblance to a spiral minaret, helping to put an otherwise universal, international building in its local historical and cultural context.

Santiago Calatrava

Early in his career, the Spanish architect, structural engineer and sculptor Santiago Calatrava (b.1951) raised the status of civil engineering through his designs for bridges and railway stations in his home country. His Montjuic Communications Tower in Barcelona (1991) on the 1992 Olympics site and the Allen Lambert Galleria in Toronto (1992) attracted significant commissions, including the spectacular City of Arts and Sciences in Valencia (1996–2005). Exploiting new technologies, Calatrava creates forms based on nature. His Stadelhofen Railway Station (1990) in Zurich features bridges and roofs above an organic, vaulted, underground arcade. His Quadracci Pavilion (2001) for the Milwaukee Art Museum, an organic, sculptural form resembling a bird about to take flight, functions as a kinetic sun-shield. One of his best-known pieces is the Turning Torso (2005) in Malmö, Sweden. Reaching 190 metres (623 ft) with 54 floors, the Torso is a twisted stack of nine pentagonal segments, each five storeys high and skewed rotationally around the central core, which is braced by an exterior steel framework.

El Palau de les Arts Reina
Sofía, Valencia, 2005

New vernacular

In the 19th century, vernacular architecture came to describe functional buildings made with local materials and labour. A century or so on, new vernacular has come to refer to architecture that reinterprets traditional forms, materials and construction techniques to suit local tastes and cultures – in part to express individuality in design, but also to avoid what has been derogatorily nicknamed 'global blanding'.

The London Olympic Velodrome (opposite, 2012) by Hopkins Architects, is clad in red cedar and designed to reflect the flowing movement of cycling. Oslo's Onda Restaurant (2010–11), designed by Norwegian firm Alliance Arkitekter, is an undulating structure of durable, environmentally friendly local pine, combined with a simple, sheer glass façade and galvanized steel gratings, while Iceland's PK Arkitektar has designed modern rural cottages with traditional timber walls and turf-covered roofs. In China, Wang Shu (b.1963) and Lu Wenyu (b.1966) mixed recycled materials and regional influences in their award-winning Ningbo Museum (2008).

Dynamic architecture

While the British Post Office Tower (1964) featured the world's first revolving floor, the world's first fully rotating high-rise building is the 15-storey Suite Vollard in Paraná, Brazil (opposite) opened in 2001, designed by Bruno de Franco. Each of the 11 floors is clad in double sheets of glass, tinted silver, gold or blue, which create spectacular effects as they rotate in opposite directions. Each floor can revolve 360 degrees in an hour. Following this concept, the Dynamic Tower (a.k.a. Da Vinci Tower) is a proposed 420-metre (1,378-ft), 80-floor skyscraper, designed by Italian-Israeli architect David Fisher (b.1949) for Dubai. As in the Suite Vollard, each floor is intended to rotate independently, with one full rotation every 90 minutes, constantly changing the shape of the tower. The Dynamic Tower will be the world's first prefabricated skyscraper, with 90 per cent built off site in a factory; only the core of the tower will be built on site. Sourcing its power from onboard wind turbines and solar panels, it should produce enough surplus electricity to power five other similar-sized buildings in the area.

Glossary

Baldachin
A canopy over an altar or throne.

Barrel vault
Also known as a tunnel or wagon vault; the simplest form of vault, resembling a barrel or tunnel cut in half lengthways.

Bascule
A counter-balanced structure; when one end is lowered the other is raised.

Bas-relief
A carving in which the design is raised from a flat background.

Bartizan
An overhanging, wall-mounted turret projecting from the walls of ancient fortifications.

Buttress
Masonry or brickwork that supports a wall. Flying buttresses are arches or half-arches that push back against a building's outward thrust.

Castellated
Finished with turrets and battlements.

Chinoiserie
An imitation of Chinese styles,

popular in Europe during the 17th and 18th centuries.

Corbels
Structural pieces of stone, wood or metal extending from a wall, serving as brackets.

Crenellations
Battlements, especially the symmetrical, geometric forms on the top of of a parapet.

Cupola
A small, usually dome-like structure on top of a building mostly on top of a larger roof or dome, and often used to provide a lookout or to admit light and air.

Duplex
A residential building divided into two separate apartments.

Entablatures
Major elements of classical architecture; the horizontal mouldings above columns that rest on the capitals.

Gambrel roof
A roof with a small gable forming the upper part of each end.

Groin vaults
Two barrel vaults that intersect at right angles.

Gypsum mortar
also called Plaster of Paris; a mixture of plaster and sand used in the construction of many ancient structures.

Himorogi
In Shinto architecture, these are sacred spaces or altars used for worship.

Hypogeum
A term usually refering to an underground temple or tomb.

Hypostyle hall
A hall with a roof supported by columns.

Keystone
A wedge-shaped stone in the apex of an arch or vault that holds the other stones in place.

Machicolations
Openings between supporting corbels in a battlement, through which stones and other objects can be dropped.

Mansard roof
A roof with four sloping sides, each becoming steeper halfway down.

Mihrab
A semi-circular niche in the wall of a mosque, indicating the direction of Mecca for Muslims to face when praying.

Mullions
Vertical bars between the panes of glass in windows.

Obelisk
A tall, four-sided, tapering monument with a pyramid-like shape at the top.

Ogee arches
Pointed arches with s-shaped curves on both sides.

Pendentives
Triangular spaces that allow circular domes to be placed on to square or polygonal bases – or rooms – beneath.

Pilotis
Pillars, columns, or stilts that support buildings, popularized by Le Corbusier.

Pylons
Support structures for suspension bridges or highways.

Quatrefoil
An ornamental tracery design of four leaves. (Trefoil is tracery of three leaves.)

Stucco
Fine, usually white, plaster used for coating wall surfaces or moulding into architectural decorations.

Tracery
Stonework elements that support the glass in Gothic windows.

Trencadís
A type of mosaic used in Catalan modernism, created from broken ceramics.

Vihara
A Buddhist monastery, originally meaning 'a secluded place in which to walk.'

Voussoir
A wedge-shaped stone in an arch or vault, either the keystone or the springer (the bottom stone of the arch).

Index

First published in Great Britain
in 2016 by

Quercus Editions Ltd
Carmelite House
50 Victoria Embankment
London EC4Y 0DZ

An Hachette UK company

Copyright © Quercus Editions
Ltd 2016

Text by Susie Hodge

Design and editorial by
Pikaia Imaging

Picture research by Denny Henke

A CIP catalogue record for this
book is available from the British
Library

PB ISBN 9781784296032

EBOOK ISBN 9781784296025

10 9 8 7 6 5 4 3 2 1

Printed and bound in China

Picture credits 9: Markus Gann/Shutterstock; 11: Jasmine N. Walthall, U.S. Army/Wikimedia; 13: Kaufingdude/Wikimedia; 15: Waj/Shutterstock; 17: WitR/Shutterstock; 19: Wellcome Images/Wikimedia; 21: The Granger Collection/TopFoto; 23: Vladimir Sazonov/Shutterstock; 25: f9photos/Shutterstock; 27: Leon Rafael/Shutterstock; 29: so51hk/Shutterstock; 33: lapas77/Shutterstock; 35: Lambros Kazan/Shutterstock; 37: Samot/Shutterstock; 39: Sharon Mollerus/Flickr; 41: Nejdet Duzen/Shutterstock; 43: martinho Smart/Shutterstock; 45: oceanfishing/Shutterstock; 47: lkunl/Shutterstock; 47: beibaoke/Shutterstock; 49: saiko3p/Shutterstock; 51: irem tural tastan/Shutterstock; 53: Tatyana Vyc/Shutterstock; 55: www.flickr.com/Flickr; 57: Marques/Shutterstock; 59: BlackMac/Shutterstock; 61: FenlioQ/Shutterstock; 63: Stefano Ember/Shutterstock; 65: Carole Raddato/Flickr; 67: Kanuman/Shutterstock; 69: Iakov Kalinin/Shutterstock; 71: SashaCoachman/Wikimedia; 73: Arena Photo UK/Shutterstock; 75: RnDmS/Shutterstock; 77: muratart/Shutterstock; 79: Paolo Costa/Shutterstock; 81: Berti123/Shutterstock; 83: canadastock/Shutterstock; 85: Claudine Van Massenhove/Shutterstock; 87: Byelikova Oksana/Shutterstock; 89: Tom Roche/Shutterstock; 91: Em7/Shutterstock; 93: /Wikimedia; 95: Zhao jian kang/Shutterstock; 97: Waj/Shutterstock; 99: photo.ua/Shutterstock; 101: Momin Bannani/Wikimedia; 103: Mohamed Mekhamer/Shutterstock; 105: Cancre/Wikimedia; 107: Anibal Trejo/Shutterstock; 109: Heribert Pohl/Flickr; 111: Robert Cutts/Flickr; 113: Anxanum/Wikimedia; 115: Natursports/Shutterstock; 117: baucys/Shutterstock; 119: Arena Photo UK/Shutterstock; 121: liquid studios/Shutterstock; 123: FCG/Shutterstock; 125: Alex Justas/Shutterstock; 127: sigurcamp/Shutterstock; 129: Gail Johnson/Shutterstock; 131: Beckstet /Wikimedia; 133: Pawel Kowalczyk/Shutterstock; 135: Louiza/Shutterstock; 137: Filippo Diotalevi/Flickr; 139: bjul/Shutterstock; 141: atiger/Shutterstock; 143: Zhao jian kang/Shutterstock; 145: Angelo Ferraris/Shutterstock; 147: Anilah/Shutterstock; 149: Marco Prati/Shutterstock; 151: Chamelion Studio/Shutterstock; 153: Filippo Diotalevi/Flickr; 155: Wikimedia Commons/Wikimedia; 157: Bertl123/Shutterstock; 159: Janis Lacis/Shutterstock; 161: Daniele Silva/Shutterstock; 163: Myrabella/Wikimedia; 165: Snowshill/Shutterstock; 167: Viacheslav Lopatin/Shutterstock; 169: Hans Geel/Shutterstock; 171: Hans A Rosbach/Flickr; 173: Anthony Shaw Photography/Shutterstock; 175: Steve Cadman /Flickr; 177: Viacheslav Lopatin/Shutterstock; 179: Volodymyr Goinyk/Shutterstock; 181: saiko3p/Shutterstock; 183: Paul Vinten/Shutterstock; 185: turbix/Shutterstock; 187: Jule_Berlin/Shutterstock; 189: Eugene Sergeev/Shutterstock; 191: Skonk Ekaterina/Shutterstock; 193: Moonik/Wikimedia; 195: Carlo Villa/Shutterstock; 197: Bertl123/Shutterstock; 199: Sergey Tarasenko/Shutterstock; 201: Steve Allen/Shutterstock; 203: JB + UK_Planet/Flickr; 205: TTstudio/Shutterstock; 207: Scirocco340/Shutterstock; 209: Alvesgaspar/Wikimedia; 211: Michael Mertens/Flickr; 213: Justin.Clark/Shutterstock; 215: Thomassin Mickaël/Flickr; 217: Anna Pakutina/Shutterstock; 219: Andrea Izzotti/Shutterstock; 221: Guilhem Vellut/Flickr; 223: Paul Daniels/Shutterstock; 225: Paul Furst/Wikimedia; 227: jan kranendonk/Shutterstock; 229: Olex Kmet/Shutterstock; 231: Dan Breckwoldt/Shutterstock; 233: Andy Lidstone/Shutterstock; 235: Claudio Divizia/Shutterstock; 237: mikecphoto/Shutterstock; 239: Alex Justas/Shutterstock; 241: Matyas Rehak/Shutterstock; 243: John Copland/Shutterstock; 245: Rictor Norton & David Allen/Flickr; 247: Wikimedia Commons/Wikimedia; 249: Dan Breckwoldt/Shutterstock; 251: Thierry Bézecourt/Wikimedia; 253: Ivan Bandura/Flickr; 255: John Copland/Shutterstock; 257: Arad/Wikimedia; 259: Muellek Josef/Shutterstock; 261: Steve Cadman/Flickr; 263: Rapomon/Wikimedia; 265: Bernard Gagnon/Wikimedia; 267: David Falconer/Shutterstock; 269: Thomas Wolf/Wikimedia; 271: Gryffindor/Wikimedia; 273: Jannis Tobias Werner/Shutterstock; 275: Wikimedia Commons/Wikimedia; 277: Chicago Architectural Photographing Company/Wikimedia; 279: Tom Bastin/Flickr; 281: Andrew Jameson/Wikimedia; 283: Chicago Architecture Today/Flickr; 285: Jeffrey Zeldman/Flickr; 289: Daderot/Wikimedia; 291: IvoShandor/Wikimedia; 293: Evan-Amos/Wikimedia; 295: kmaschke/Flickr; 297: David Kasparek/Flickr; 299: Georg Slickers/Wikimedia; 303: Thomas Cloer/Flickr; 305: Jean-Pierre Dalbéra/Flickr; 307: Husky/Wikimedia; 309: Mike Reiss/Wikimedia; 311: cdschock/Flickr; 315: Dreizung/Shutterstock; 317: Pinotto992/Wikimedia; 319: Timothy Brown/Flickr; 321: Esther Westerveld/Flickr; 323: Gubin Yury/Shutterstock; 325: frm_tokyo/Flickr; 327: Javierpuertonico/Wikimedia; 329: Jeff3000/Wikimedia; 331: m-louis/Flickr; 333: Robert Pernell/Shutterstock; 335: jphilipp/Flickr; 337: Los Angeles/Wikimedia; 339: Zache/Wikimedia; 341: Carol M. Highsmith/Wikimedia; 343: Fgrammen/Wikimedia; 345: Javier Gil/Wikimedia; 347: Nezdezda Zavitaeva/Shutterstock; 349: Aleksandr Zykov/Flickr; 351: February Desnu/Shutterstock; 353: Chris 73/Wikimedia; 355: Capture Light/Shutterstock; 357: Christine Zenino/Wikimedia; 359: Richard George/Wikimedia; 361: Edwardx/Wikimedia; 363: Zack Frank/Shutterstock; 365: leoplus/Flickr; 367: cate_89/Shutterstock; 369: Steve Morgan/Wikimedia; 371: TungCheung/Shutterstock; 373: monysasu/Shutterstock; 375: 663highland/Wikimedia; 377: Rob124/Flickr; 379: Michielverbeek/Wikimedia; 381: José M Blanco/Wikimedia; 383: Iain McGillivray/Shutterstock; 385: Tupungato/Shutterstock; 387: chrisdorney/Shutterstock; 389: ~Pyb/Flickr; 391: srgpicker/Flickr; 393: Maximilian Dörrbecker/Wikimedia; 395: Loz Pycock/Flickr; 397: claire rowland/Flickr; 399: Sardaka/Wikimedia; 401: Dominic Scaglioni/Flickr; 403: vincent desjardins/Flickr; 405: Samantha Beddoes/Wikimedia; 407: Radamés Manosso/Flickr;